"I couldn't put it down! It's engaging, funny, unpretentious, and beautifully captures the trials and tribulations, the lows but also the highs of finding one's voice as a writer. Marianne Gingher is a perfect-pitch storyteller—and not because she's Southern! We who are writers know what hard work it is to weave her magic, and how the ultimate magic is to make it look easy and fun. This memoir will be a godsend to young and not-so-young writers struggling to believe in their work. Marianne Gingher not only tracks the writer's journey from first-grade assignment to first novel, but actually tracks a whole generation from the '50s onward, our coming-of-age, on the page and in the life!"

—Julia Alvarez, author of *Saving the World*

"Marianne Gingher's hilarious account of her literary apprenticeship contains the same stellar qualities that make her fiction so engaging: wit, grace, wisdom, sparkling and lissome prose, and a refreshingly unjaded and joyful appreciation of mystery, both on and off the page."

—Michael Parker, author of *If You Want Me to Stay*

"*Adventures in Pen Land* succeeds on several levels: as a memoir, as a meditation on an emerging aesthetic, and as a guide to the writing life. Gingher's tone is witty, vivid, intimate, and optimistic. She is able to treat herself lightly without deprecating her own process and career. This is a fine book, which offers up extraordinary descriptions and insights on every page."

—Trudy Lewis, author of *The Bones of Garbo: A Collection of Short Stories*

Adventures in Pen Land

Adventures in Pen Land

One Writer's Journey from Inklings to Ink

Marianne Gingher (signature)

Marianne Gingher

University of Missouri Press   Columbia and London

For Randall
With much admiration
and gladness you're among
us xo Marianne

Library of Congress Cataloging-in-Publication Data

Gingher, Marianne.
  Adventures in pen land : one writer's journey from inklings to ink /
Marianne Gingher.
    p. cm.
  Summary: "Candid memoir that takes readers along on a tour of soul-
sucking jobs, marriage, a teaching career, '60s pop culture, writing work-
shops, and other amusing detours on the way to publication, sharing keen
insights into the process of novel-writing and the role of a southern writer in
American literary culture"—Provided by publisher.
  ISBN 978–0–8262–1817–9 (alk. paper)
  1. Gingher, Marianne. 2. Authors, American—20th century—Biography. 3.
Authorship. I. Title.
  PS3557.I494Z46 2008
  813'.54—dc22
  [B]   2008022253

♾™ This paper meets the requirements of the American National Standard
for Permanence of Paper for Printed Library Materials, Z39.48, 1984.

Designer: Jennifer Cropp
Typesetter: Foley Design
Printer and binder: COLORCRAFT Ltd., Hong Kong
Typefaces: Berkeley Book and Demian

    The author wishes to thank Fred Chappell for permission to reprint an
excerpt from his poem "Gold and Mean," from *The World between the Eyes*,
Louisiana State University Press, 1971.

    The first eleven essays in this volume appeared serially, in slightly altered
form, in the *Rambler Magazine*, beginning with vol. 2, no. 6 and running consecutively through vol. 4, no. 4 (November/December 2005–July/August
2007).

To Lawrence,
for everything,
I O U

Contents

Acknowledgments

This book might never have been written were it not for the intrepid Elizabeth Oliver and her husband, Dave Korzon, founders, editors, and publishers of a little gem of a Chapel Hill magazine, the *Rambler,* who invited me to write a series of stories (originally titled "A Woman at Work and Play") about the evolution of my writing life. They stuck with me for two years. The first eleven chapters of *Pen Land* ran consecutively in the *Rambler* from November/December 2005 through July/August 2007. The editors' enthusiasm and meticulous stylistic advice enriched every page.

I'm immensely grateful to my first and most ardent reader, Lawrence Naumoff; to my mother, Betty Jane Buie, who made sure I told the truth—or at least its more comic version (I have changed a few names to protect the eminent); to my pal and fellow writer Debby Seabrooke, with whom I've shared life stories every Friday morning over coffee for years (most recently at Simple Kneads Bakery in downtown Greensboro, where mere whiffs of the cinnamon buns have kept us sane and off the harder drugs); and to my brave, talented, and inspiring sons,

Rod Gingher and Sam Gingher, a Peace Corps volunteer and pianist, respectively; to Daniel Wallace for his jaunty cartoons, and to Fabienne Worth, a writer herself and *Rambler* subscriber, who wrote the best fan letters I've ever received.

I'm indebted to friends and colleagues in the Department of English and Comparative Literature and the Creative Writing Program at the University of North Carolina at Chapel Hill for camaraderie, encouragement, jokes, and wisdom, especially Susan Irons, Bland Simpson, James Thompson, Daphne Athas, Ruth Moose, and Michael McFee. Thanks to Jane Danielewicz, Laurie Langbauer, and Lawrence Naumoff for sharing my work with their classes.

For their sparkling company, abundant goodwill, and friendship, I thank Mark Buie, David Buie, John Buie, Rebecca Carrel, Esther Hughes, Greta Medlin, Barb Bennett, Jill McCorkle, Sarah Dessen, Courtney Jones Mitchell, Jenne Herbst, and Fred and Susan Chappell—always.

I am lucky. I teach at a wonderful public university that supports the arts and humanities. Final preparation of this manuscript was completed during my tenure as a Chapman Fellow at the University of North Carolina's Institute for Arts and Humanities. Thanks to the Max C. Chapman family for their generosity and vision.

Adventures in Pen Land

One

My Writing Life Begins, Age Six

My writing life begins with a whopping lie I tell my first-grade teacher. It is a calculated and dramatic lie, a lie with an agenda. I will not be punished for it or suffer a shred of remorse. On the contrary, I will be rewarded. Mine will be a long uphill slog toward artistic integrity, achieved only decades later, but the lie—fiction begetting more fiction—will have started it all.

I am six years old. It is 1953, and my best friend, Pam, has gotten a *Ding Dong School Book*. I'm about to detonate with envy. I want a *Ding Dong School Book* more than I have ever wanted anything, more than I want Pam's new Madame Alexander doll, which she brings to school and asks me to hold for her during recess so she can ride the merry-go-round. While she is spinning, I rub the doll's peachy face in the playground cinders, but Pam is so dizzy when she climbs off the ride that she doesn't notice that the doll has developed an irreparable case of acne. Why did I do such a thing? I am still so astonished by this memory that I can even recall the weather conditions that hovered over all (it was a brilliant cold and sunshiny day with a cloudless cobalt-blue sky, the kind of heartless sky that often accompanies funerals; just the sort of day the devil likes because the shadows are so richly dark that he can hide in them; pleats of heated air rippled over the chimney tops and you could smell the gruff, dragon breath of furnace-fired coal). The legacy of my memory is that along with the good, I can recollect every bad or hostile thing I ever did: memory as comfort and joy, memory as penitentiary complete with torture chamber.

The television show *Ding Dong School* predates *Mister Roger's Neighborhood* and *Sesame Street* by many years. A baggy old woman in a black dress hosts the show. Her name is Miss Frances. She is always seated, like Whistler's mother. She wears her hair in a bun, low on her neck, and she is deadly serious about fun. She reads stories with the gravity of a child psychologist. She works sock puppets and draws pictures. There is something she talks about called a *Ding Dong School Book,* and this must be my first brush with advertising that really penetrates. She holds the *Ding Dong School Book* up to her viewers and describes the hours of fun it will provide.

This is no ordinary coloring book. It's a revolutionary version of the form because every page is *blank.* There are no drawings to color in, no printed riddles, no find-the-squirrel-hidden-in-the-picture sorts of activities. The stark idea of blankness fascinates me. Like an unmarred patch of snow you're compelled to step in, blankness unfurls its maverick opportunities, open invitations to the stampede of invention. I am wild for its permission.

At school, Pam shows up with a *Ding Dong School Book* tucked under her arm, and she lets me hold it, open it, flutter the abundant, soft newsprint pages, sniff them. They smell a little bit like oatmeal. Every one is dazzlingly blank, as promised, except for the *Ding Dong School* logo in the upper-right-hand corner. It's a bell with a handle, tilted as if it's ringing. I'm a little disappointed about the bell. No matter what you draw, there's always going to be a bell in the upper-right-hand corner, advertising *Ding Dong School.* If you draw ghosts drifting out of a haunted house, there will still be that stupid bell, reminding you it's just a picture you've made, not a fantastic world you've slipped into. Nevertheless, I do not rub the *Ding Dong School Book* in the playground cinders. It's the seed of an illuminated manuscript and I accord it all due respect.

Pam loves to draw like me, but she is neater about it. I admire neatness and try to copy it, but I'm a catawampus girl. My shoes are always gobbling up my socks. My fine hair tangles. The hemline of my skirt droops where I've kicked out the stitching playing acrobat. I get impatient coloring between the lines and I scribble. You ruin things if you scribble. Pam doesn't scribble. She is methodical and precise. She doesn't ever break the tips off her crayons. Her red crayon—everybody's favorite—is saved only for coloring the lips of beautiful princesses and queens. If it breaks in two or has to be peeled, Pam asks her mother for a whole new box of crayons.

When we spend an afternoon drawing, our favorite subject is graveyards. We have a formula. Take a sheet of Blue Horse notebook paper and turn it on its side so that the vertical red margin line runs horizontally across the bottom of the page. Take your pencil and trace over the red line and you have the foundation for the graveyard. It's a flat graveyard, no hills. Scribble it green and you have unmown grass. Color it *neatly* green and you have freshly clipped grass. Draw the tombstones on top of the line, as many as you can fit in. Some can be plain crosses, some arched, some—for rich people—look like castle turrets.

The fun part is deciding who is dead. If you're mad at somebody, like your brother, you can put a real name on a tombstone. Or you can do celebrities like Davy Crockett. Write the birth and the death dates on in pencil. Draw flowers that loved ones have placed on the graves. Make up stories about the funerals and who came and what sorts of diseases and accidents people died from.

Sometimes when Pam and I are lying on the floor of her living room, on our stomachs, drawing, her brother, Scott, shows up. He's about five years older than us, an oafish sixth-grader and a saboteur. I'm scared of him because Pam's scared of him. The best thing to do is not to speak to him, no matter if he pretends to be interested or nice. The first word or two that pops out of his mouth might be nice, but it's bait. He's waiting to egg you with bully words. He's always scowling and sulking and dragging his feet. He'll try to stomp a foot on our graveyard pictures if his mom isn't nearby. Mostly she's always around, like a prison matron, only pretty and kind. Her voice is buttery Southern soft, and when she reprimands Scott she doesn't shout because Scott knows that if he disobeys her he'll have his father, Ted, to reckon with. Ted is an older version of Scott and built to last.

Scott is the first critic of my creative life, the threat of his monstrous disregard lurking on the periphery of my artistic jubilee.

Pam's a better drawer than me because she is patient. I want to rush through my drawings because new ideas keep crowding my head. Her work is methodical; mine is all flurry and smudge. But as we advance in school, my drawing gets better than Pam's because she stops drawing.

She gets bored with it. She decides to be good at kickball instead or arithmetic or boys. By seventh grade she will be so good at boys that she will have left me for dead.

I am grateful to Pam for liking to draw as much as me, in the beginning. I don't yet have the sense that making art can feel lonesome or require you to go off by yourself for long periods of time. In the beginning, art is a social activity the same as lunch or recess. We both have plenty of confidence about it because our parents regularly compliment our efforts, and neither of our mothers ever complains about buying us new crayons. Which is why, when Pam's mother buys her a *Ding Dong School Book* as a reward for suffering through a dental appointment, I think I'm due a reward too. But I can't just ask for a *Ding Dong School Book*, can I? I have to *deserve* it for being brave or enterprising.

"But you don't need to go to the dentist," my mother reminds me when I ask. Dr. Pringle had filled two cavities about a month ago. Besides, Dr. Pringle has his own system of rewards for stoic children: plaster-of-Paris sculptures of Snow White and Cinderella, Bambi, all seven Dwarfs, Tweety Bird and Sylvester, Bugs Bunny and Elmer Fudd that he crafts himself for a hobby. There are hundreds of them, perfectly white, about the size of big saltshakers, lined up on his lobby shelf, for young patients to browse while their Novocain wears off. I think of the statues as ghost toys. You can't really play with them because they chip and crumble. They are to look at, collect, and admire, Dr. Pringle says, beaming. And you want to be able to do exactly that, because they're good for nothing else. When you hold one, it makes your hand go numb and dull with carefulness.

Pam and I both adore Mrs. Johns, and we are her teacher's pets. She likes Steve Blackwood, too, and sometimes, she lets Steve take a nap on her fur coat. The fur coat is a nice, silky place to take a nap, if you're sleepy, but Pam and I are never sleepy at school. We like keeping our eyes open or else we might miss something. We take turns during rest period, when all the other students have to put their heads on their desks and go to sleep for thirty minutes, giving Mrs. Johns back rubs. She puts her head on her desk and shuts her eyes, and we swirl our little fingers across her back. It is very relaxing and makes us calm and quiet too. I am glad that I don't have to sit next to Pee Wee, who smells like boy-spit, or Sonny Fine, who drops pennies on my lunch tray because he thinks I am his girlfriend. I throw the pennies away with my cafeteria trash. Sometimes during the school day, just thinking about some of the boys I don't like and the whiny girls and the dizziness of the playground merry-go-round and maybe a scab I got from falling off makes me lonesome for home.

I have a brainstorm one rest period when I am rubbing Mrs. Johns's back: the brainstorm is that I am probably sick and will need to go home. I'm not sure I can make myself cry, but I am going to try. I lean close to Mrs. J.'s ear and I say, "I feel sick, Mrs. Johns."

"What's the matter, dear?"

"My ear." The notion of an earache comes instantly to me. Maybe because of Mrs. Johns's ear that I leaned so close to whisper in. Her ear looks like it might hurt. She has taken off an earring so that she can rest her ear on her arm, and where the clip of her earring mashed her earlobe, the skin looks red and dented.

"You do feel a little feverish," she says, pressing my forehead with her wrist.

"I want to go home."

When she rocks me, because of her kindness and her lack of suspicion, I begin to whimper. The more she soothes, the easier it is for me to feel sorry for myself, to believe that maybe I really am sick because how could a child fool somebody as smart as Mrs. Johns? I even manage to feel a little sorry for Pee Wee, who is not as clever as me or a teacher's pet and must live with the smell of himself day and night, and for my mother, who trusts me to tell the truth and will be worried when Mrs. Johns calls her to come pick me up. I'm having an empathyfest. I feel sorry, too, for Mrs. Johns for believing me when I don't deserve it. At some point I squeeze out a tear or two, but the tears have the pressured flimsiness of obligation, and they are tiny, not the big great dollops of grief I am known for when I cry with honest gusto.

Normally I'm a clown and Mrs. Johns lets me be. I take the chalkboard erasers, thickly pollinated with yellow chalk dust, and I powder my face and slant my eyes by pulling the corners with my fingers and jabber chipmunk Chinese; sometimes on the playground, I'll take a flying leap and land my skinny little self into Mrs. Johns's arms, clamping my legs around her waist and singing, "A monkey wrapped his tail around the flagpole!" She always laughs.

In a little while my mother arrives. I sniff her lively perfume, trellised like flowers among the soft fibers of her coat along with the fragrance of stern autumn air and acorns and the sunshine that warmed her hair. Her hair is the color of butterscotch. She lifts me from Mrs. Johns's lap where I have been clinging, more like an invalid than a monkey, and she takes me straight home and tucks me into bed. I sleep in a big double bed in a sunny room with two windows. My bedroom walls are a deep salmon pink. Over the bed hang dreamy paintings of Jack Frost and the Man in the Moon and Jack Be Nimble, and I am afraid of them sometimes at night because Jack Frost wears pointed boots and has a chin as sharp as an icicle, and Jack Be Nimble is not afraid of fire, but I am, and I worry that some night he will land in the candle flame he's jumping over and burn up. The Man in the Moon grins like a kidnapper. We all have been told about kidnappers and are more afraid of them than anything in the world, even the inky slinking creatures under our beds.

Mother bundles me into my big clean bed and plumps up my pillow and takes my temperature. "Good," she says. "It's normal." You'd think she'd be disappointed. All that trouble of bringing me home and it turns out my temperature is normal. She tells me to rest. It is the hardest thing in the world to rest when your temperature is normal. "Can you think of anything you want right now?" she asks.

Without hesitation, in my frailest Little Match Girl voice, I suggest that, strange as it might seem, a *Ding Dong School Book* would help tremendously to cheer me up.

By Christmastime, I have filled up every blank page, writing stories with pictures. The only words I know how to spell with confidence are "oh" and "no" and "look," because Mrs. Johns drew eyebrows over the double O's to make them resemble eyes. Mostly I draw each story, page by page, in the *Ding Dong School Book* and recite each one aloud, following the illustrations. I have memorized *The Night before Christmas* and so I illustrate the entire poem. Next, I illustrate *Goldilocks and the Three Bears* in voluminous detail. Then I branch off and write an original story about a pair of rabbits who get married. There is a picture of the rabbit wedding. I draw the rabbit house, which is shabby and makeshift—I think it's actually a hotel flophouse

"Then, one night, something terrible happens."

because there are numbers on the doors—until the rabbits fix it up. They wear regular clothes. Father rabbit wears a necktie; mother rabbit wears high heels and lipstick. There are baby rabbits. Then, one night, something terrible happens. A thief slips in and stabs the mother rabbit to death. The father rabbit finds her lying in a pool of scarlet blood—which I doubtlessly drew so passionately with my red crayon that I either broke the tip or wore it down to a nub and had to peel the paper. There is a funeral, and even the rabbit mourners' car is crying big splashy blue tears. The car looks like a Studebaker. I think the father rabbit remarries, because, on the last page, he is looking pretty recovered; he's bought a new cruise ship of a car, a Lincoln Continental perhaps, and a new house with fancy kitchen appliances, and he is smiling and has the print of a new woman rabbit's lipstick kiss on his cheek.

My mother, amused by the story, shares it with my dad. It's probably significant that his nickname for her is "Bunny" and her nickname for him is "Rabbit." If parents back then had been as dependent on psychologists as parents of my generation, I might have been put on the couch. The story clearly owes its subliminal origins to my overhearing arguments between my thrifty mother and my extravagant father, who was always trying to slip the purchase of a new automobile or some fancy gadget past her.

For a six-year-old girl in 1953, there is no art critic or overly zealous English teacher to analyze this rabbit story and condemn it as melodramatic or ridicule its theme. There is no editorial authority to shame my unscrupulous suggestion that material possessions can distract bereft rabbits from sorrow or to declare the tale vastly shallow, or without moral value, and ludicrously simplistic. Nobody tries to speculate about *what's wrong* with Mr. Rabbit, if he snaps back from tragedy so quickly and spends all that money with a grin on his face? Shouldn't that make him a suspect in the murder?

My readers are simply charmed. When they lift their gazes from the story, they're smiling. Imagine! Nothing but gung-ho *approval.* It's enough validation to make one a storyteller for life. On the last page of my *Ding Dong School Book* I neatly and correctly write "the end" and feel immensely satisfied.

Two

A Mole's Diary

It's 1959. America is not at war with anyone, and, with the annexation of Hawaii as our fiftieth state, the nation seems to move ever closer to Paradise. "Everything's Coming Up Roses" plays on the radio. On a goodwill tour of the world, President Eisenhower stops in India and is welcomed by millions of cheering citizens and hailed as the "Prince of Peace."

Meanwhile, I'm galumphing around Kiser Junior High School as a new seventh grader and not feeling the least bit peaceful. Skin-and-bones tall, my hair barbered short with Prince Valiant bangs, I'm at war with who I've been conscripted to be. Whose idea is it that I should look like a boy? My mother won't allow me to wear lipstick to school until I turn thirteen. I argue that it's crucial for me to wear lipstick so that people can determine my gender. My eyes are gobbed up with glasses; my teeth are gobbed up with braces. Nobody can tell what I am beneath such a load of remediation. Plus, an orthopedist has prescribed corrective shoes to treat my pronated ankles. Instead of cruising school in flimsy, debonair loafers like my friends, I'm wearing a pair of big brown clunky tie shoes. They make me look like the dumbbell in some fairy tale who goes to the baker's to buy two loaves of bread and wears them home on her feet.

But the worst thing about junior high—a crowded, impersonal hothouse of paranoia filled with glaring teachers—is feeling anonymous. My respected elementary-school reputation as a novelist and playwright dwindles to nothing but a dead weight upon my heart.

I'd written and staged four plays before I graduated from Sternberger Elementary School—each with twenty-five speaking parts. My most recent production, "The Case of the Missing Mummy," featured a character named Professor Spitty Spat who began every sentence with "P-P-P-P-P-P-Personally," spitting on all who shared the stage with him. The actors victimized by his spray reeled backwards in paroxysms of disgust, provoking much hilarity in the audience. The primary-grade students especially loved Professor Spitty Spat, and the boy who played him enjoyed, postproduction, a bit of celebrity around the hallowed halls of good old Sternberger. But at Kiser, this same boy looks mortified every time I wave hello. He has put away all childish things, like spitting on people to get a laugh, and he doesn't need some freak from his past—is it a girl or a giraffe or a ladder wearing glasses coming towards him?—reminding him of some inanity best forgotten.

Eventually I get the message: at Kiser Junior High School it is no longer cool to be a writer. Writers are about as cool as bald-head babies. Worse. All the writers in our language arts textbook are *dead*. What *is* cool, what all my old pals are struggling to do, is to invent a slick new identity that will help you survive. Not to worry if some of the new identities seem like personality disorders.

I am learning that survival always takes precedence over art.

Finally it's Thanksgiving. That year, like every year in my poky hometown of Greensboro, North Carolina ("Greens*boring*," my oldest brother, Knothead, will dub it during his hippie years), we eat Thanksgiving dinner across town at Granddaddy and Grandmother Ruth's house on Kensington Road. I'm at an impatient age for lingering after the meal. Nor do I care much about holiday food, short of admiring the big glossy turkey, which, for all its grandeur, suggests the collision of pomposity with bad luck as my grandfather stands over it with his carving knife. Somehow I never think of the turkey as being completely dead until Granddaddy settles its hash and divvies it up. The large table is set with fancy china and draped with a lace cloth. We all sip iced sweet tea from the tall wedding glasses that have the date of my grandparents' nuptials etched in the wavy glass: May 24, 1916.

After dinner, the air feels balmy from cooking and the continuing friction of Grandmother's busy to-and-fro. Her small kitchen is a tumult of eggbeaters, mixing bowls, pot holders with burnt, crusty edges, damp tea towels slung on countertops, footprints and skid marks in a snow of flour on the floor. In the den, the television murmurs news of a football game that seems to have been in progress for years.

While the women tidy up, Granddaddy sits with my father, his only child. The world of the men is a slower, digestive world. "Hello, Mole," my father says to my grandfather. "Hello, Mole," my grandfather replies. "Are you in your hole, Mole?" Daddy asks. "The mole is in his hole," the old man says. They have always called one another Mole, after a comic-strip character that they like and chuckle over. Mother says it's the only thing they ever agreed was funny.

Mole Senior smokes a pipe and rests it in a beige pottery ashtray that's made to look like a pond surrounded by a crocodile. The crocodile has bumpy skin that I like to stroke. Its tail loops the border of the ashtray and disappears slitheringly over the side.

The den glitters with windowpanes and pine paneling splashed with sunlight. It's a cozy mole hole where everybody likes to congregate. But if you're a kid, you have to be enterprising to keep yourself amused. On a scalloped table sits a pedestal candy dish with a glass top. It's usually filled with butterscotch balls wrapped in squares of yellow cellophane we children press on our eyelids and wear like sunglasses. It makes you glad the world isn't totally yellow. There's a pine cupboard with whatnot shelves filled with trinkets and figurines, lots of china slippers, some fancy and some plain. I imagine that one green glass high-heeled pump came from the Emerald City. I'd give anything for a pair of them to wear to school in place of my brown tie-shoe galumphers. I stick the delicate little shoe on my finger and walk my finger around like a foot.

My grandparents don't keep toys, except a bunch of junk in a caved-in cardboard box on the floor of the hall closet. There's a leather ball, deflated, a metal horse, a metal tractor, a metal locomotive without wheels, some weathered wooden blocks. These were my father's toys in the 1920s, and so what if they're probably valuable antiques, they bore us. There are dominoes and decks of old playing cards and two decrepit board games that we sometimes play: Crokinole and Parcheesi. All the games

"It doesn't exist except in my head."

smell like tattered library bindings on grimy, dog-eared books. The cards are soft and humid.

My brothers have gone outside to run around. Mostly, when I'm finished being useful in the kitchen, I mill about the house and look at things, lamenting the lack of sources of fun in the lives of my grandparents. Why does my grandmother seem content to dart from chore to chore? How does my grandfather sit perfectly still in his chair with an ottoman, doing *nothing*! He never loosens the tie he always wears, never kicks off his shoes. Maybe he *is* the chair with an ottoman. I hug him when I visit, and he stoops to accommodate me, but he doesn't hug back. He pats my shoulder. He steps carefully around us children as if we are spinning tops, and then he sits down. Of everybody I've ever met, I believe he's the most boring person in history. He makes me think of somebody in mythology slowly turning to stone.

At twelve, I believe that boredom and boringness are the worst fates that can befall a person, even worse than disease, and that the only antidotes are invention and bustle. For me, invention is a survival tactic, an involuntary muscle kicking back at what's dull, letting *me* know I'm alive.

I can't help making things up when I'm bored: plays, stories, drawings, games. Their lifelines unravel effortlessly from my brain. I even invent a way to keep my friends from being bored when they come to my house on a rainy Saturday. My strategy is to drag out a book I call *The Book of Things to Do.* It doesn't exist except in my head. We're sitting around, bored flat as old chewing gum mashed on a shoe. We are so bored that unless somebody thinks fast, we are going to lapse into comas. It's hard to think fast when you're bored, though. Your mind feels like a finless fish floating in sludge. I gaze up at the living room bookcases that display the spines of my father's medical textbooks and the book club selections he and my mother have collected over the years. The book club books have lackluster titles like *Sincerely, Wallace Wayde, The Old Gray Homestead, The Velvet Doublet, Rascal's Heaven,* and *The Robe.* But as I stare at them through the sludge of my near-coma, one thick red book with blurry gold letters looms forth and offers itself as a trove of coma-dispelling advice.

"What's that?" Pam asks as I pull the book from its shelf.

"It gives valuable suggestions of things to do so you won't be bored," I say.

Pam smirks.

"The title says *Holt's Childhood Diseases,*" Sandra points out.

I pay the naysayers no mind. Then, as I flutter the tome's pages, a little panicky now that I've promised some coma relief, to my astonishment, ideas for entertainment begin to flow. I have hit upon the jackpot of ad-lib, first cousin to the magpie's bluff and whatever trickery, self-delusion, or desperate jibber-jabbering free fall of thought that dissuades creative writer types from writer's block.

"The book says that rainy days are good for riding bikes. It says: 'Tie umbrellas to your handlebars, *chickens*! Pretend you're rickshaw drivers and have to work rain or shine.'"

While they mull over the possibility of such an activity, I'm inspired to make other suggestions, flipping the book's pages. Soon nobody's in danger of a coma, and we're all playing at something because a brainstorm is contagious.

It's still Thanksgiving 1959. It is going to be Thanksgiving 1959 for all eternity. The dishes are done, the crumbs swept into the dustpan. I've walked around and looked at things. I've watched my grandfather's stillness until I feel that I am turning to stone, too. I've put on my coat, hopefully, waiting for deliverance. But the adults seem to have grown roots where they sit. The ball game drones. My grandmother is busy with a needlepoint project; my mother is copying her recipe for "Strawberry French Cream Pudding." My brothers are running around in the backyard, their coats thrown over bushes, their cheeks aflame with cold. They are playing dodgeball with the squashed, flat ball from the box of nontoys. There are no children in the neighborhood for me to play with, just lots of elderly people living in tall somber houses with swept sidewalks and neatly raked yards hedged in nandina bushes. Across the street, behind a chain-link fence, lives a ferocious German shepherd named King that we are not allowed to visit. I believe that King only barks and snarls because he's bored. I feel like barking myself, but then my parents would send me outside to play dodgeball with my rowdy brothers and that stupid flattened ball from yesteryear.

I amble upstairs and sequester myself in one of the guest rooms to read my father's old *Oz* books. The fluffy gravel of the chenille bedspread pits my elbows and knees as I leaf through *Ozma of Oz,* my favorite. Sitting on Princess Langwidere's dressing table are a number of different beautiful princess heads from which she can choose. Every morning, she picks out not only her attire for the day, but her head. Oh, the possibilities of an ever-fluid cosmetic identity! The heads twist on and off easily, like turning doorknobs.

Reading makes me want to write in the same way that a whiff of chocolate makes me salivate. If I go downstairs and ask my grandmother for paper, she will hand me a single sheet of her good gray vellum stationery. One sheet. She can't imagine the pinched, uninspiring boundaries of such an offering. I need room to blather and to illustrate, so inevitably I'll pilfer one of Daddy's doctor's prescription pads from the glove compartment of our car. The prescription pads have little square munchkin pages, but they are plentiful.

On the Monday after the longest Thanksgiving in history, Mother sits on the edge of my bed before my alarm goes off for school. "Wake up, sweetheart," she says kindly, over and over. "I want you to be fully awake because I have some sad news. Your grandfather died last night."

Suddenly, with her words, my old stone-faced grandfather is not boring anymore. I keep waiting to cry, but I don't. I try to cry, but I can't. I had burst into tears when our cocker spaniel ate poison and died. But I knew our dog better: I had played with him. I won't feel sad about my grandfather's death until the funeral, when we sing "A Mighty Fortress Is Our God" to a thunderous organ and I glimpse my father crying for the first time in my life.

"He got up in the middle of the night and went into the bathroom," my grandmother tells my father, her voice small with wonder. "Then he came back to bed, laid down, gave a little sigh, and died."

All the adults marvel at the peaceful way he died. "If I could choose how I'd most like to die, I'd simply go to sleep and fade away like your grandfather," my mother says with the gentlest tone of envy I've ever heard. It may be the closest she's ever come to complimenting him.

I miss the familiar place he occupied in our family as senior Mole, the bulwark of him, his distinctive silence. I am nostalgic for watching him carve a turkey one more time. I feel guilty for not having paid him more attention during his last Thanksgiving with us, but I think I experience the loss of him as missing an opportunity rather than a person.

Not long after, I come into possession of the little red leather diary, purchased at a Boots Pharmacy in England, that my grandfather kept during World War I, beginning in 1917. The diary, written entirely in a lovely filigree of pencil, easily fit inside his shirt pocket. His hat and glove and shoe sizes are carefully recorded, and his affiliation with the Second Scottish Rifles, BEF France.

He leaves New York on October 8, 1917, aboard the HMS *Baltic* of the White Star Line. The passage to England takes approximately two weeks with a landing in Liverpool.

Nov. 17: Was called out of bed to see Lt. of R.F.C. who was dying. His sweetheart came to see him often during his illness, always bringing flowers.

That year, there is no mention of Thanksgiving. By December, the weather turns dreary with "plenty of ice and snow and dampness and very dark nights." There's no mention of Christmas.

Jan. 27: Was orderly officer today. Went to bed with bilious headache.

Jan. 28: Not feeling well all day—had three degrees of temperature at night. Air raid on London said to be the worst on record.

Mar. 20: Returned to Leeds.

Mar. 21: Left Leeds to return to London to go to France. Expecting air raid. News of big offensive in France arrives.

Mar. 25: Got gas instructions today and received and tested gas mask.

Mar. 26: Was sent to base hospital no. 7. Gave anesthesia all P.M.

Mar. 28: Started for the front in an ambulance train this A.M. Interesting trip. Slept on ground with only one blanket.

Mar. 29: Arrived at S—in P.M. and went to B—. Very hungry on arrival. Heavy artillery action in progress. Came back to S— at night.

Mar. 30: Very busy all P.M. Got to bed at 5 A.M. Rained most of day—mud everywhere. Pitiful to see old French women and children trudging in the rain and mud with a few bundles of clothes on their backs.

April 6: Inspected 400 new draft men. Found three with scabies, four with measles.

April 10: Marched to R—a distance of 14 miles and billeted for the night in an old chateau built in the 13th century.

April 11: Marched to D—and went into billets. Lots of men had to fall out on account of sore feet.

April 16: *Marched 4 miles out to seaside for rifle range practice. One man's rifle exploded, blowing off two of his fingers.*

May 11: *Went out to front line trenches. Heavy shelling by Germans in A.M. Fragments of shell fell all around aid post. One man in C company missing. Only part of one leg found.*

May 12: *One man fatally wounded. Name Barnes. Age 19.*

May 18: *28 Men gassed by mustard gas. Some made blind. Three killed and 12 wounded.*

May 20: *Had bath today and came back to trenches near Avion.*

May 21: *Had 15 gassed cases today. No wounded. Very hot in trenches. Had three letters from Ruth.*

On May 24, he had been married two years. There is no mention of his anniversary. The diary continues through December, again passing over Thanksgiving and Christmas without commentary. Countless entries note only "the usual routine" or "nothing new today." He tends soldiers felled by Spanish influenza as well as wounds and mustard gas. He is summoned to a French village to deliver a baby. "Baby born at 4 AM. Nice fat baby boy." Every two or three weeks he reports that his troops receive hot baths and clean underwear and have their uniforms disinfected. The weather is always remarked upon when most severe: cold and mud and rain in the trenches seem more intolerable than heat.

It will take reading Hemingway, many years later, to make World War I dramatic for me, but for now, my grandfather's red diary glows in my palm like a remnant of *The Book of Things to Do*. It's a little jewel of permission to fill in the blanks: *Reimagine your grandfather.* And so I do. I uproot him from his armchair life where he seemed content to reach no further than the lamp beside his chair for all the light he needed. Now I can picture him striding bravely across the world, far outpacing me in his aware-ness of what it means to be alive and to matter. He's wear-ing a filthy uniform, not corseted in his Sunday best; he's delivering a gloriously squawking French baby amid the ruins, not passing docile plates of turkey. He's comforting a dying soldier, sleeping in mud, going hungry, working sick, marching his sore feet over the land, all without com-plaint, carrying on and on and on. In spare moments, he is jotting down this diary of bare-bones dispatches that don't begin to tell his whole story, but almost, astonishingly, do. It's even possible, if you read between the lines, that he turns out to be somebody's hero.

Of course I am still a galumpher at Kiser Junior High School. Some things don't change, even when somebody in your family dies. But by the time I discover the diary, I'm a ninth-grader, and on my way to a better life. I have decided not to write plays anymore. Plays depend too much on the participation of my grudging junior high conscripts to bring them to life. So I move on to solo projects: I'm writing love poems, having saturated myself in Shakespeare. We've just finished studying *Romeo and Juliet* in Mr. George B. Hellen's English class. Who am I writing love poems to? To any boy who wants me, of course. And none of them do. Sometimes as I write, I imagine that I'm pining for my sweetheart soldier far away, conjuring the aching distance we all strive to close, even in times of peace, between what we long for, what eludes us, and what we can actually have. But deep down in my unopened valentine of a heart, I know that what I'm trying to feel is a frilly imitation of the real thing. I know I'm still an amateur at life and love.

My grandfather didn't have to imagine what being separated from my grandmother felt like. On the last page

of his stoic little no-nonsense diary, in a minute filigree of
sharp pencil, he copied these tender lyrics: "Nobody else
knows how to cheer me / Nobody else can nestle near
me. . . . Though my lips don't tell you so / Gaze in my
heart and you will know / There's nobody else but you."

"How many of you have ever lost somebody dear to
you?" Mr. Hellen asks the class during a discussion of
Romeo and Juliet. We are all still such baby-heart innocents
that I may be the only one who raises my hand.

Three

The Silencing of the Lamb Faces

It's 1964 and I'm sitting in Miss Peggy Joyner's AP English class, word-drunk as usual. I've been researching the love affair between Robert Browning and Elizabeth Barrett for my term paper and have glutted myself on *Sonnets from the Portuguese* and the letters that flourished between the two smitten writers. I've begun to write a few sonnets myself. Miss Joyner passes out one of her weekly vocabulary lists to help us prepare for the SATs, and I eagerly scan its offerings: *cacophony, mellifluent, aesthetic, tantamount, pulchritude, malfeasance, timorous, tintinnabulation.* But what normal person walks around inserting such marvelous sounds into ordinary speech? People from a more eloquent, word-centered century, that's who. I picture consonant-lean men wearing top hats and shouldering capes, women fluttering plumed fans at their delicate lily-stem necks. I imagine sabotaging myself socially with a public comment like, "The cacophony in the cafeteria today is tantamount to aesthetic malfeasance." If

"Ah! A mellifluent tintinnabulation!"

you want to actually *use* these words in real life, best to slip them into poems that are destined to be thrown away, like this regrettable fragment from my incompletely lost sonnet about a pianist:

> In *pulchritude* his soul of music grows
> And nourished by sincere *aesthetic* loves
> He plays a *mellifluent* tune on rows
> Of *tintinnabulating* keys. O, gloves
> Could never warm his *tim'rous* hands so well . . .

Freddie, who sits behind me, taps my shoulder. She wants to know who I'm writing my term paper on. Her father is a college chancellor, and she's destined to cut a brilliant swath herself in the groves of academe. She spits on the grave of Elizabeth Barrett Browning for being a frail second-rater of a poet, actually more a *balladeer* than a poet. Everybody in our AP English class knows that a balladeer is on the level of Mr. Bojangles, not Keats. "Don't you find her love poems *sappy*?" Freddie asks. I will never again hear the word *sappy* in quite the same way. I will hear the "yellow-bellied *sap-sucker*" version of the word. As if sentiment is a form of cowardice. Meanwhile Freddie is writing her own term paper on something like "Einstein's Theory of Relativity as Applied to Metaphor."

Freddie serves as literary editor on our high school yearbook staff of which I am a new recruit. My job is to write copy that describes the meritorious deeds of campus service clubs. It's a boring assignment because the clubs themselves are boring, populated by a slew of candyasses and pious do-gooders. Besides, when I write, I get squirmy when straitjacketed by inflexible facts. She taps me on the shoulder again. "While we're on the subject of writing," she says, and passes me the article I'd turned in to her about some club's wildly successful sale of doughnut holes. "Needs *tons* of revision." But that's not the worst of it. Written across the top of the paper in a tonnage of red ink is one word: *CRUMMY.*

Perhaps it's a gentler wrecking ball of a word than, say, "miserable," "filthy," "cheap," or "worthless," but as I take the paper, I feel pulverized. CRUMMY: a trifle built of crumbs, half-baked or it wouldn't be crumbling apart, of no more value than a pellety little pile of cockroach fodder. CRUMMY. I know of no more dismissive word in the language of literary criticism. Well, maybe "sappy."

More about Freddie later.

That spring, as we await college acceptances, my friend Janet Turner and I, encouraged by our parents, sign up to take vocational guidance tests at Saint Andrews Presbyterian College in Laurinburg, North Carolina. We're hoping to learn whether our ambitions coincide with our talents. Unlike Janet, who was voted "Most Likely to Succeed" and whose range of abilities makes narrowing her options seem like clipping her wings, I'm spared the confusion of broad choice. I'm only good at two subjects: art and writing (Freddie's opinion notwithstanding). The vocational guidance tests will tell me, once and for all, whether I should focus on art or English in college, simple as that. Meanwhile, I've honed my sonneteer's skills, experimenting with both Italian and Elizabethan forms, under the pen name Angela Farrington. I have no idea where the name Angela Farrington springs from, but the two initials—A and F—suggest icons of success and failure, the extremes of judgment to which I submit my writing. Either I'm excellent or I'm crummy; mediocrity is not a possibility. It's all or nothing.

Lately, I've gushed forth a compulsive kind of autobiographical prose, too, in which I document in detail my life as a preener, daydreamer, wallflower, and malcontent. The previous summer I'd kept a journal titled *Saga of My Seventeenth Summer,* which I wrote entirely in green ink, often by candlelight while listening to the orchestral tsunami of Rachmaninoff on my stereo. Completed, the tome weighed in at over four hundred pages. *Saga of My Seventeenth Summer* was all about slouching toward something wonderful—in masculine form and preferably a sensitive poet type—in order to illuminate my reason for being.

Tests, schmests. Who are we fooling? The real reason Janet and I are eagerly driving to Laurinburg is to indulge in the lark of a road trip, a chance to stay unchaperoned in a tourist home, to smoke cigarettes if we're so inclined, to break curfew and cruise for boys. The phrase "tourist home" sounds subversively itinerant and makeshift. All we know about Laurinburg is that it's a small college town halfway to the beach, which makes it a good hundred miles closer to romantic possibilities than home.

My mother loans us her sporty gold Chevrolet, and Janet and I roar off into the sunset, the radio blasting Sam the Sham and the Pharaohs singing "Wooly Bully." I'm possessed by the luminous certainty that I love to write and the tests will prove I'm good at it, that an intellectual snob like Freddie can't squelch my desire, that Janet and I are going to have the time of our lives in Laurinburg, and that freedom feels precisely like writing, an unspooling of oneself not only toward significant discovery but also a sense of amplitude. I yearn to hang my wooly bully head out the window while I drive because I feel like blowing in the wind, whichever way the wind wants to blow me. I don't yet feel shadowed and cramped by my ignorance, but it's lurking in the here and now, waiting its chance to have at me.

When it shows up in your life, ignorance feels a little like the guest you'd never invite but who aims to crash the party anyhow. I've come to think of pure ignorance as the shaggiest, most unshaven, unkempt form of political incorrectness, before shame's gotten the chance to slick it up and teach it some manners.

In 1965, I have the nerve to think of myself as a poet, and yet I remain ignorant of poems by James Dickey, Robert Lowell, Sylvia Plath, and Elizabeth Bishop. I know nothing of Flannery O'Connor's work or Eudora Welty's *Thirteen Stories* or Katherine Anne Porter's collection for which she wins the Pulitzer Prize in 1965. The critical celebration of recent books by James Baldwin, Kurt Vonnegut, Saul Bellow, the praise for Jerzy Kosinski's *The Painted Bird* will elude me for the time being. If anyone mentions Tom Wolfe's *The Kandy-Colored, Tangerine-Flake Streamline Baby*, I assume they're quoting Beatles' lyrics. Significant contemporary books are not yet on my radar. When I leaf through my parents' *New Yorker*s, I only read the cartoons. No teacher or friend will recommend current newsworthy authors to me, but, too ignorant to find them on my own, I will delight a while longer in my zealous aspirations unimpeded by humility.

By the time we arrive in Laurinburg it's rainy and dark. We hadn't planned for rain. Now our hair's going to frizz or go limp. We'll have to cruise for boys with the windows up; if we smoke, it will stink up the car. The proprietor of the tourist home tells us that there is, indeed, a curfew. If we aren't inside by eleven o'clock, we'll be locked out. The good news is that smoking is allowed. There are Bakelite ashtrays in our bedroom.

We unpack our travel cases, take showers, spiff up. It feels like we're dressing to go out. Out with whom? Whatever boneheads Destiny throws us. We're a mere hundred miles from the beach, so close we can almost smell the salt jingling in the air, the suntan lotion on the handsome suntanned skin of boys. As I recall, it's March— not even beach weather at the beach. Never mind. Just the word *beach* seems twenty degrees warmer than most other words.

We drive up and down the main street of Laurinburg— which is about three stoplights long. Is it really the main street? It can't be the main street because nobody's on it. We stop at a service station to ask. A weary, grease-stained attendant nods, yes, it's the main street. He fills our gas tank and checks the oil. Is he a teenager? We can't quite tell. Is he cute? We can't tell that either. Maybe he's cute, but maybe he'd be cuter if he cleaned up. We buy some inferior hamburgers because there isn't yet a McDonalds in Laurinburg. We cruise up and down the main street for hours in the rain. We keep the windows up, but we smoke anyway, pulling from a pack of Kent cigarettes. I try to teach Janet how to inhale, but she's no good at it. We drive back to the service station to buy Cokes and to see if the attendant is cuter than we remembered. We have been revising him in our collective memories. How cute does he have to be? Compare him to some of the boys we know at home and he may come out cuter than we first thought. When we pull up in front of the service station it's raining harder. The Coke machine is inside, so one of us is going to have to get wet. The wet one will have ruined her hair. The dry one, with her hair still in place, will have the advantage if the attendant is interested. We decide that it won't be fair to the wet one and that maybe the attendant isn't cute after all and that our imaginations are fried with desperation.

Back in our dreary little room with the lumpy double bed and mismatched furniture and bare-bulb ceiling-light fixture with a pull chain, we get ready for bed. We lie side by side in the dark, listening to the swish of going-nowhere traffic. I am thinking of the Bakelite ashtrays and what a waste not to have used them, but just the thought of smoking another cigarette makes me want to throw up.

Saturday morning, Janet says she feels hungover from all the cigarettes. But we rally and drive over to Saint Andrews for the tests. It's a brand-new college, a cluster of nouveau Williamsburg buildings that still smell of fresh paint. A fuzz of recently seeded grass struggles to grow into a campus; sapling trees cast dainty spindles of shade.

Inside the building where we take the tests—the School of Education or, perhaps, of Psychology—we are greeted by a guidance counselor–type woman in a skirt and blazer, with tightly permed hair, the face of a smiling lamb, a soft, damp handshake.

The first test is an IQ test—they can't fool me. The counselor woman acts apologetically secretive about it. I'm not allowed to see the results. Is she protecting me from finding out that I'm a mental loser? She whisks the IQ test away and gives me some sort of test that will quantify my knack for proportion and design. But I can't stop worrying about the IQ test and how it was booby-trapped with all these stupid puzzles. I hate puzzles. I worry that the counselor woman is going to grade my IQ test and break the news to me that, frankly, no matter how well I do on the other tests, I'm not college material.

Here comes another test: What would you rather do? (a) Be a shoe salesman, (b) March in a military parade, or (c) Drive an ambulance. Who do you admire most? (a) Politicians, (b) Clowns, or (c) Sock manufacturers. Which is the most fun? (a) Writing a letter, (b) Changing a lightbulb, or (c) Working a puzzle. Well, *that* one's easy. Writing *anything* is more fun than *anything.* But if it turns out that I'm not college material, maybe I'd be happier as a shoe salesman. I actually checked that box.

Mid-afternoon, our battery of tests completed, Janet and I are summoned for individual conferences. A second lady counselor with a smiling lamb face materializes and beckons Janet to follow her while I go along with the first one into a clean, bright office.

Okay. Turns out that Freddie was right. This is what the lamb face says to me: "You'll have a bright future in art or design. But an English major? No way, kiddo. Baa baa black sheep! Your writing sucks."

Of course, she didn't say that. It was 1965 and nobody used the word *suck* unless they were talking about a lemon or doing something through a straw. But I got the message: I might as well have written in lemon juice rather than pencil for all my evaluators cared. Which would you rather do? (a) Slide down a mile-long razor blade into a pool of alcohol, (b) Read Marianne's writing, or (c) Suck roadkill through a straw. Best to go with (c).

I go off to college and *double*-major: art for the lamb faces, English literature for me. I come by my stubbornness naturally. My parents are stubborn people, in different ways, but stubborn nonetheless. My father pouts when he's being stubborn; his bottom lip sticks out further than a school bus bumper. My mother stops talking to everybody when she's being stubborn; you could go to Antarctica and back in the time it might take her to thaw.

It's the fall of 1966 and I'm a college sophomore. I got through Dr. William White's composition class at 8:00 A.M. three mornings a week the previous year with a C and remain undaunted. Never mind that on the first writing assignment he gave me a D and mimeographed the paper for the entire class to critically heave-ho at. "The diction is so appalling in this paper," Dr. White told the class, "that it appears as if the writer referenced a thesaurus instead of a dictionary." Busted.

My dormitory, located at pilgrimesque Salem College in Winston-Salem, North Carolina, thumps with Beatles music from their album *Rubber Soul.* From somebody's room Herb Alpert blows his horn, which competes with the ferocious harmonies of the Mamas and the Papas, Simon and Garfunkel's "The Sounds of Silence," the Beach Boys, the soundtrack from *Dr. Zhivago.* It is not cool to listen to "The Ballad of the Green Berets," but that song's a big hit now that Vietnam is heating up. Every sophisticate I know wants to see Elizabeth Taylor and Richard Burton verbally assault one another in the controversial film *Who's Afraid of Virginia Woolf?* Best-selling books include Truman Capote's *In Cold Blood,* Jacqueline Susann's *Valley of the Dolls,* and Masters and Johnson's *Human Sexual Response.* This year the Pulitzer Prize in fiction goes to Bernard Malamud for *The Fixer.* Anne Sexton wins a Pulitzer for her volume of poetry *Live or Die.* Literary critics tout the avant-garde: Pynchon, Barth, Coover, and the quirky Southerner Walker Percy. Do I hear about any of them? No. At Salem College, my study of literature begins with *Beowulf,* Chaucer, Shakespeare, and Milton and ends with the Victorians. At Salem, the Victorians are considered *modern.* Still, in fits and starts, the lid on my ignorance is starting to lift.

My art professors mock Norman Rockwell, whom I have always admired. Sure, he's sappy, but he's an excellent painter. No, they say. No, he paints commercials for an America that doesn't exist. He's an *illustrator.* They say it like it's a dirty word. Don't I get the difference? They ridicule Leonardo da Vinci too. What they're actually ridiculing is the Mona Lisa's popularization. She's as recognizable worldwide as McDonald's golden arches. The Big Moan, they call her. You'd think she was the only painting Leonardo ever painted. They have a poster in their office of the Big Moan that they throw darts at. They admire the Pop Art of Andy Warhol, Roy Lichtenstein, and some sculptor named Tony Smith who calls in an order for a steel cube to be built and delivered to the front of a museum, installed and painted by lackeys. He never lifts a finger except to write his name beside the manufactured box. I'm in an outrage about art all the time, but Professor Shewmake thinks that's the healthy response. Art isn't art unless it provokes, he says. True art would just as soon give you a heart attack as not. Professor Shewmake takes our painting class to a gallery where there's a series of blank canvasses, framed and mounted on the wall. "But they're all *blank*," I protest when he pauses in front of one of the canvasses and snickers with appreciation. "It's the *idea*," he says, pitying me, I can tell.

At lovely, leafy Salem College, we are cordoned off from grimy politics and the rumblings of war protesters and civil rights activists. Black Power is introduced into the civil rights movement, clarifying the split between the pacifist followers of Martin Luther King Jr. and militants Stokely Carmichael and Floyd McKissick. Not a single black student attends Salem College. There are no black faculty members. We've all grown up as privileged daughters of a segregated South. Sometimes the college seems like a mounting board for butterflies.

New words pop up: glitch, flower child, abort, acid rock, psychedelic, hawk, hippy, LSD, miniskirt, mod, Third World. For the first time there are stereo cassette decks, tape cartridges, plastic bank-issued credit cards, the rare and endangered species list issued by the Department of the Interior. The National Association of Broadcasters instructs all disc jockeys to screen records for hidden drug references or obscene meanings. Jimi Hendrix helps to popularize the electric guitar. Everything's in flux and tumult: the good, the bad, the ugly, the sad, corporate, boutique, beauty, duty, tolerance, and overthrow.

As a sophomore, I am taking a demanding British literature course taught by ancient professor Jess Byrd—so old she looks barnacled—as well as Dr. White's class on Victorian prose. I've offended Professor Byrd by writing a paper on *King Lear* in which I submit that his tragedy is due less to the conniving of his daughters than to his senility. How insensitive of me. Professor Byrd returns my paper with the dismal grade of C. The vision of a lamb-faced prophet hovers over me, a reinvigorated genie of doom.

In Dr. White's 8:00 A.M. class—he's obviously a morning person—I struggle to stay awake. Matthew Arnold's prose is killing me. It's like reading cinder blocks. Then, one morning, we're supposed to discuss Thomas Carlyle's *Sartor Resartus.* It's the last straw. I've stayed up all night just trying to make sense of the first paragraph. This isn't literature; it's physics. I mope into class, open my book, and sag over it. I hate Thomas Carlyle more than I ever hated puzzles. Admitting this, I realize that it's probably time to quit my English major. You win, Freddie. You win, Lamb-face Counselor. You win, Dr. William White of the dried-up word-lust. You and your smug praise of dictionaries, when any true writer knows that the thesaurus is where word lovers go to feel happy as pigs in a wallow.

Dr. White stands primly at the front of the room, not yet niched behind his lectern. He hasn't opened his grim little copy of *Sartor Resartus.* He's still got on his overcoat and the porkpie hat he wears to protect his bald head from the cold. Is he having some sort of breakdown himself? Maybe this most recent rereading of *Sartor Resartus* has ruptured a few of his brain cells too. "We won't be discussing Carlyle today," he tells us. "We're going to the library to hear a guest speaker instead."

Shockorama. This is the most irregular announcement I've ever heard made at Salem College. Classes are never suspended, cut short, or interrupted for any reason. I imagine the guest speaker as some dignitary who will lecture us about Thomas Carlyle in an even haughtier, more prune-faced tone than Dr. White's.

As we set out on the short walk to the library, I have no idea that my souring outlook on literature and life is about to dramatically change.

A beaming librarian introduces the speaker as Sylvia Wilkerson, a North Carolina novelist. *Sylvia Wilkerson*, triple meter, a dactylic poem of a name. Lithe and beautiful with long dark hair cascading down her back, Sylvia Wilkerson is only a few years older than me. She wears a simple scarlet shirtwaist dress and black flats; her eyes are bright, her profile bold. She looks haunted with idealism like Joan Baez. But the most marvelous thing is the book she holds in her hands because she wrote it. A girl holding her own book, not Thomas Carlyle's, that's what I see. It's astonishing. I may be dreaming. Nope. There sits Dr. White. No way I'd put him in my dream. I watch him though, Mr. dictum of the dictionary. He is watching Sylvia Wilkerson read her fiction too, and he is *smiling*. It's not a smug, sneering smile either; it's a smile of approval. It's like old Dr. White can't believe his good fortune either: that a vibrant young woman has written a novel and we are listening to her read from it and she is not a ghost from Literature Past. My heartbeat is as close to tintinnabulation as it's ever been. And there's not a beach or a boy in sight.

Many years after, thousands of pages of my own writing later, in the fall of 2004, I'm reading e-mails in my campus office and up pops an inquiry. Frieda Somebody is writing to tell me that she is a fellow at a prestigious national institute for scholars located near Chapel Hill, where I teach. How am I and what am I up to? Could we meet for lunch or dinner? Please write back.

Frieda. *Freddie*! She's become a highly respected, even

renowned, literary theorist and has taught at Berkeley and Johns Hopkins. I know her by her luminary's reputation, not her writing. Her work is still higher math from my perspective. I imagine her brilliant treatises on "Logarithmic Function in the Works of Thomas Carlyle" or "Fraudulent Fractals in Elizabeth Barrett's Proofs of Her Love for Robert Browning."

For several days I do nothing. I don't respond. How easy it would be to erase the e-mail and get on with my life. I imagine meeting her at a restaurant, sitting across the table from her powerful scrutiny. I hear the squeak of my small talk against the roar of her erudition.

I'm a mature woman, a professor with tenure for goodness' sake. What's my problem? I suspect that I'm not alone among creative writer types who scuttle the halls of academia feeling vaguely apologetic for not having thoroughly read and appreciated *Sartor Resartus*. Add to that deficiency that creative writers have the audacity to presume that yet another poem or story is *needed* in a world already chockablock with literary treasures. On any campus, you can pick out the poets and novelists from among the scholars. We've got the mischief-making, rumpled, scabby look of Cub Scouts rather than the spit-and-polish of Eagles with their pile of scholastic merit badges. What we offer sometimes seems as vain and elective as liposuction. Every day in college classrooms, new theories about, say, Thomas Carlyle glisten urgently like plump fresh donor hearts, awaiting transplant to rejuvenate the canon. If you teach in a big, smart English department like I do, you tend to do a lot of genuflecting to all those *real* doctors.

When I finally respond to Freddie's e-mail, it's due not to a surge of confidence but to curiosity. I just can't help myself. Who is she now? Does she wear power suits and butch her hair? Is she fat? Vegan? Did her heart ever soften toward Elizabeth Barrett Browning? I doubt it, but who knows? Nearly forty years have elapsed since she eviscerated my writing life with the bloody scythe of a single word. By some trick of largesse, I begin to think of her as a character, and, like all characters, open to the possibilities of revision. If I meet her and hate her, I can always put her in a short story as a murder victim.

On a dark and blustery November night, I arrive at the Lantern Restaurant in downtown Chapel Hill and take a seat at the bar. The room is narrow and lacquered black; crimson and yellow Japanese lanterns blossom above a murmuring clientele; curlicues of smoke unraveling from cigarettes float into the dark like shape-shifting hooks and question marks. The place looks like something out of a Raymond Chandler novel. Maybe somebody *is* about to get murdered. I tell the bartender that I am meeting someone I haven't seen in almost forty years. "Cool," she says. "Think you'll recognize her?"

Good question.

But I do recognize her.

A dainty, dark-haired woman in a fashionable tan trench coat enters the bar. She gently shakes her umbrella, then, smiling broadly, proceeds forthrightly in my direction. After all this time and dread, it's her expressively alert face, her smile, that I remember best. How could I have forgotten that despite her tartness, she was always as eager as a lamb face to be friends?

We move to a table, order food and wine, and launch our reunion. If she's ever read one of my books and found it lacking in the way that Einstein might be bored with long division, she gives no clue. She describes her beloved father's long illness and death, her gratitude that my father had been his physician. She recalls her husband's scandalous affair, their divorce, the difficulties of raising a child as a single parent, her professional challenges, and her nostalgia for the South. She doesn't want to talk about her successes. It's her heartaches and losses that she deems worth a story. We are two women telling about our lives; reflecting on the ironies, absurdities, and choices; crediting the good fortunes that have brought us to this moment; and, yes, commiserating about some of the crumminess that abounds *off* the page in real life. But we've survived, even flourished; we lift our glasses in mutual salute. If this were fiction, nobody would buy such a tidy, sappy ending. But in reality, what's not to like?

Four

The Art Teacher

It's mid-August 1969 when I report to the first of a string of teacher workdays preceding my first job. I'll be teaching art at North Forsyth High School off Shattalon Drive in rural Forsyth County, near Winston-Salem. I am wearing the most conservative dress I own, a gold sleeveless polyester sheath, my swirly married monogram, MBG, branded across the bodice. Because of the humid North Carolina heat I carry the prissy matching jacket. This was my official "going-away" suit as a bride. I don't know why riding off into the sunset as a newlywed required dressing as primly as a bank executive in those days, but I don't think I was the only bride who, in her last public appearance before the honeymoon, looked as chastely sealed in her clothes as a legal contract in a business envelope.

I've been married two years, and the gold suit is still the nicest conventional outfit I own and, most important, not a miniskirt, and therefore guaranteed to make a good impression on my first day as a sober professional. I am

Booger

no longer merely a callow college girl with pie-in-the-sky dreams of becoming a poet.

In spite of the ghastly heat, I'm wearing stockings. They feel like Saran wrap attached with glue. I'm also wearing my only pair of high-heeled pumps: tortoiseshell patent-leather shoes that my mother bought me at Montaldo's, the last expensive and truly *nice* shoes I believe I will ever own, since my husband and I are so poor. Why am I wasting their beauty, wearing them to work where they will get scuffed and downtrodden? They have none of the mule-esque qualities of schoolteacher shoes; they are lady-go-to-luncheon shoes, and they look a little indignant at having been made to slum in the environs of a working girl. Mother would say that I am *hacking* them.

My husband and I live on shabby Academy Street, not too far from Old Salem in Winston-Salem, where we rent for seventy-five dollars a month (approximately a quarter of his salary as a middle-school English teacher) a cracker box of a plain brick house with no stove or air conditioner. The weeds in the yard are hip high. The neighbor on one side of us is an old crone we call No-Teeth who owns a dog named Booger. Our neighbor on the other side, Pearline, keeps a gorilla for a boyfriend who is fond of knocking his fist through the window of her front door in the middle of the night when she throws him out. If he hollers and cusses enough, Pearline relents and lets him back in. Afterward I can't get back to sleep for the percussion of them making up as relayed by the antennae of weeds that stand trembling between our two units.

Meanwhile, in lieu of a stove, I've patched together an efficient lineup of wedding gift appliances along the kitchen counter: a toaster oven, a toaster, an electric frying pan, a blender, and a single-burner hotplate. I'm not bothered by the arrangement since I don't really know how to cook. Anyhow, it's been too hot to cook. Because of the sweltering summer heat, we've finally acquired a MasterCard and bought 18,000 BTUs' worth of air conditioner. Once installed, the gargantuan unit looks like somebody drove an army tank through our kitchen window. It was between buying an air conditioner or a stove. A no-brainer, really. But that's how we're living: no-brainer to no-brainer, with the help of a MasterCard.

Soon we will become a couple with two incomes. But since I won't get my first paycheck until the end of September, I can't imagine any financial easement, only my inevitable trip to the grocery store at the end of the month, where, with our bank account running on empty, I'll write an iffy check for the food I know how to fix: cans of beans and cocktail wieners for beanie-weenie, cheese for grilled-cheese sandwiches on fluffy, cheap Sunbeam bread, eggs, bacon, ground beef for hamburgers, and canned tuna. Looks like we are edging towards the Atkins diet before it was even invented.

Mid-August, a certified teacher, twenty-two years old, on my way to my first day of *salaried* work, I feel a bit like I imagine a grazing animal must feel when snatched from

another. "I'd just as soon die if she was one of mine. Her hair is completely white."

"It's all that marijuana she and what's-his-name smoked," the first woman says gravely. "It'll do that. Turn your hair white as a granny's overnight."

The principal has stopped his spiel about bus duty and cafeteria supervision and hallway patrol and bathroom inspections. He glares at our table until the gossips retreat from their huddle and straighten up. I fear that in his mind, because of my proximity to them, I will forever be lumped with the inattentive. Already I imagine Mr. Snavely opening my personnel file and recording a demerit.

The good things about teaching art: there are no papers to read and grade. No take-home work. Sure, it's messy and labor-intensive while you're doing it, but once the brushes are washed and put away, the materials reshelved, the tables sponged off, you're done. Your brain is still word-fresh, so you have energy for writing in the evening after you've eaten your beanie-weenie. The trick of writing after you've worked all day is to have a job that saves your word skills stamina. Teaching high school art doesn't require a lot of words, spoken or written. Just a tolerance for mess, confusion, insult, humiliation, boredom, self-doubt, the constant undermining of your ideals, and the awful realization that art matters, on a conscious level, to about one young person in a thousand.

The bad things about teaching art: Scooter Boone and Bubby Suggs, venetian blinds, Miss Clydesdale, and the teachers' lounge.

Scooter Boone and Bubby Suggs, two hulking, slack-jawed rednecks, sit across from each other at a wobbly table in my second-period class. They look a little crazy in

FART

the eyes. Is it the marijuana, or were they born that way? Seizing the advantage of the table being wobbly in the first place, they tip it back and forth like a seesaw. Bubby likes using the linoleum tools because he can imagine their potential as weapons. He lifts them toward the overhead fluorescent lights and turns them slowly, like a maniac butcher obsessed with sharpness, watching the blades glint. I play Beatles music in class to calm the savages while they work, and one tune, "Maxwell's Silver Hammer," finally inspires Bubby to gouge out an interpretation in his gray square of linoleum. In the cheerful little song, Maxwell takes his silver hammer and bashes his teacher's brains out.

Scooter Boone won't do art of any kind. He calls it "fart." He lopes around the room, bothering people, breathing on the necks of the earnest one or two students bent over their fart projects. He has smirking, wet, pouty Elvis lips and a surly, moist, dark curl plastered to the middle of his forehead like a snail. He wobbles the table extra hard on purpose to mess Bubby up when he's cutting his linoleum design. He's hoping Bubby will stab himself with the gouger and bleed all over himself. That would be so funny. Both of them talk and laugh about what a funny dumb-ass thing it would be if Scooter made Bubby slice off a finger. Har-har.

One day Scooter brings a baseball bat to class, and he and Bubby corral me with it in ring-around-the-rosie fashion. I'm trapped, huffing and puffing with failed bluster. I'm too young to be their teacher, still hoping to puncture their bad-boy armor with some strategic, pointed kindness. I don't yet believe in their pure, raw evil, so I don't know how to combat it. I just stand there, dumbfounded and inept. Round and round they go, besotted with loutish power, holding on to the baseball bat, predatory leers on their faces. They don't even see me anymore. Once it's caught, a hapless animal is just quarry to them. I stand there, shrinking into subhumanness, waiting for them to crash the bat on my head and put me out of my misery. That's really the truth of it.

Six weeks into the semester I make an appointment with Mr. Snavely. The situation with Scooter and Bubby is not an isolated problem, but it's the direst. Daily I boot some troublemaker out of class who boomerangs back in.

Mr. Snavely's office is so shipshape you expect his window to be a little porthole. It makes me seasick to be there, like I'm about to walk the plank. On his desk, two sleek pens are snubbed at precise 45-degree angles into desk-set holder sockets, not some tawdry mug. His elbows rest on an ink blotter without one blot. Every few seconds he smoothes over the blotter with his hand as if to perfect its blotlessness. There's a bronze nameplate with his name engraved, lest one forget, and a glass paperweight without any papers to weight. The walls of the office are sand-colored cinder block. No art on display. No family photographs. Nothing to soften and humanize the blazing beige blankness. The floor is beige tile over concrete slab, no rug. There are a few plaques and certificates on the wall, proof of degrees and citations of honor that landed him in this position of authority. But with his burr-cut hair, his crisp, short-sleeved white shirts, and his black pants with sharp creases, there is less of the swaggering bully about him and more the spit-and-polish military officer. Besides banning slacks on women, he mandates that men keep their hair trimmed short. Beards and mustaches—popular at the time, especially among the counterculture—are nixed. He orders the black basketball coach to pare down his Afro.

But as far as I observe, there is no counterculture within the teacher population hired by the Winston-Salem Forsyth County schools anyway. People here aren't signing teaching contracts to shake up the status quo. The school-system administrators have enough problems on their hands dealing with mandatory desegregation and student unrest and snotty parents and white flight to hire the edgy and outspoken, the rabble-rousers.

I'm counterculture, only I don't look it or even know it yet. But sitting in Mr. Snavely's office, my job confidence shrunken to the size of one of Scooter Boone's spitballs, I feel subversive, as if I'm only marking time in this place. It's nowhere I'd want to hang my hat or join the circle or sing along for very long. It's bleak. Mr. Snavely's tidiness is as bleak as the chaos I face every day in class. I thought I needed his advice to help me clean up my act, but his tidiness feels even more lonely than my mess. Mr. Snavely gazes at me like I'm threatening to besmirch his blot-free blotter, and I feel so tiny sitting there that I'm betting I've forgotten how to tie my own shoes.

"I'm glad to have this opportunity to speak with you," he says. His eyes avoid mine. He's staring hard at the space beside my head, kind of like a squirrel does, sizing you up. A squirrel will point its face at you but pretend it could care less by not hitting the bull's-eye with its gaze. "It's all about the venetian blinds, the problems you're having with these boys."

"The blinds?" Is Mr. Snavely stoned?

"Before you leave your classroom for the day, remember to furl the venetian blinds, all of them, at half-mast. We want a uniform look at every window."

"Yes, sir."

"Every day since school started, you've forgotten. I leave the parking lot, and when I glance back at the school, which I always do, out of habit, I see all the venetian blinds lowered at half-mast except in the art room. Looks sloppy, lady."

"I didn't realize. I'll take care of it. Sorry, Mr. Snavely."

"One kind of sloppy leads to another, if you get my meaning, lady."

I nod.

"You understand now what's expected? The trouble it can cause and influence? Wanted to give you fair warning that I've let teachers go for just this sort of thing."

"Disciplinary problems?"

"Not adjusting their venetian blinds. What have we been talking about?"

In the wake of the venetian blinds reprimand, I go home to find that the publisher Dodd, Mead and Company has returned *The Remarkable Barkable*. There's a little rejection note that's the size of a sheet of toilet paper inside. It's signed, and when I lick the signature the ink runs. A genuine signature usually heartens me. But today I need more; I need a sign that my talent lies elsewhere than in the regulation furling of maladjusted venetian blinds.

My husband suggests that we go to Crown Drugstore down the hill for some hot dogs. It would cheer me up not to have to cook supper, he says. But I do not want cheering as much as I want some Great Talent Scout in the Sky to validate me. *We can't afford to go out to eat,* I tell him. It's hot dogs, not lobster, he says. *We have to pay for the air conditioner first,*I snit. *And the alligator loafers with tassels you bought yourself.* (I'm still smarting over his latest MasterCard charge. The alligator loafers cost as much as a month's rent.) *Just because we have two pitiful salaries,* I shriek, *doesn't mean we can live like profligates!* What did I tell you about harping on the money thing? Is it worth it? No, it's not, he says in a chilly Mr. Snavely tone of warning. He unfolds a five-dollar bill from his wallet and lights it with a match. See? We're five dollars poorer now, and does it matter? Will we miss it? Not in the long run.

I slam a Bun-O together for my supper. You take a bun, slam it with a tomato slice, slam on a square of rubbery American cheese, and slam it with Bac-Os, which scatter when they're slammed. Bac-Os are some kind of fake bacon bits that look like scales of grated shoe leather shined with oxblood polish. You shove the whole shebang under the broiler in your toaster oven and turn up the heat. Sometimes the fat in the cheese sputters and ignites and the inside of the toaster oven catches on fire. You can watch everything burn through the little glass window. Burn, baby, burn.

When I return to North Forsyth, I'm both inept *and* angry—it's a bad combination. There's nothing worse for law and order than somebody who's mad and powerless. I rip the soda-pop Beatles off the turntable in my classroom and plunk down the hard stuff: *Hair,* the seriously raunchy rock musical I'm crazy about. I light a few sticks of incense, too. I'm going to the dark side now, and I'm taking my students down with me.

It's 1969. The world's lost its innocence and gotten plenty snarly—I'm just a late bloomer playing catch-up. In the recent movie *Easy Rider*, a couple of marijuana-huffing hippies riding choppers get blown away by a redneck with a goiter in his neck. In my mind, the goiter is all that distinguishes the man from Scooter Boone and Bubby Suggs. That same year I wait in line over at the Janus Theatre in Greensboro to have my ID checked by police to gain admission to the Swedish film *I Am Curious (Yellow)*, the first mainstream movie to contain male frontal nudity. I *am* curious. Joke's on all the prurient, because the movie is mostly a chattering satire and boring beyond belief unless you follow Swedish politics. The nude scene is saved until the final frames. People fall asleep in the theater waiting for it, snoring like chain saws.

In 1969 sex and death are always making the headlines. Best-selling novels include Roth's *Portnoy's Complaint*, Puzo's *The Godfather*, and Nabokov's *Ada, or Ardor*. Cult leader Charles Manson and his followers are charged with the murder of pregnant starlet Sharon Tate and four others. Vietnam has killed off nearly 40,000 American soldiers to date and ten times that many enemy troops.

For all the controversy surrounding lyrics from *Hair*, some of its songs, like "Good Morning, Starshine" and "Aquarius," play every day on the radio. But on the soundtrack of the original Broadway show, which I play for my class, there is lots of profanity, antiwar sentiment, flag-burning bravado, and paeans to wildly free love. There's that ticklish song about fellatio and cunnilingus, true, in which "pederasty" rhymes with "nasty," and white girls sing about black boys tasting delicious, like "chocolate covered treats," not to be outdone by a ravenous-sounding chorus of black girls who offer a tribute to savory white boys. I can remember thinking, well, that's the sort of unbiased admiration of our opposites that we hope integration achieves, right?

In class on that day of my insurrection, we are lofted on a tide of song, curious and mellow. Nobody's misbehaving, and for once I'm not watching the clock because time, like a hip conductor, is jiving us along here at the fart class penal colony. Suddenly, in the little glass observation window of my door, a poisonous face appears. It's either a cobra or Miss Clydesdale, the living Old Maid card, who teaches English next door. She wears her hair pulled back so masochistically into a bun that her eyes bulge from the sensation of self-scalpage. Her glasses dangle around her neck from a cord that possibly doubles as a lynch rope. Her tongue is forked. Okay, I made that up. But her sweater hangs at her shoulders from the clench-fisted little clamps of a sweater guard that look bully enough to beat somebody up. They are doing some serious knowledge-mongering in her English class, like diagramming complex sentences, and our music, thudding in such unfortunate proximity, is scrambling their clauses and dangling their modifiers.

"What is going on in here?" Miss Clydesdale shrills when I crack open the door. "What's that *smell*?" I can tell by the alarmed expression on her pasty face that she thinks we're smoking pot. "How dare you!" she says to me, and I realize that she's misidentified me as one of the students. "Where's your teacher?"

"You smell incense," I tell her. "I *am* the teacher." But she's already wheeled away, charging down the corridor like a SWAT team of one, her high heels drilling on the tiles, her silk scarf billowing, as she full-steams-ahead to report my insurgency. The brisk frictional *shwftshwft* of her pantyhose sounds like somebody rubbing two sticks together to start a fire.

Miss Clydesdale

The summer before, sitting in Mary Jarrell's living room as she turned the pages of *The Remarkable Barkable*, I'd felt nothing but a sprawling, dumb, slaphappy, privileged ebullience about life, about art. Mrs. Jarrell smiled almost tenderly as she read. Sometimes she laughed at something I didn't know was funny. *The Remarkable Barkable* was about a stray dog who couldn't bark. He toted a metropolis, filled with friendly fleas, on his back. One day Mayor Phineas Flea's daughter crawled down the dog's throat to determine what was wrong with his barker and got stuck. The dog finally rescued her by *barking* her out—BOOM— like a person shot from a cannon. Turns out he could always bark; he just needed a reason.

I knew nothing of the conflagrations of the writing life then, nor much about life, period. I was like some well-intentioned doofus daughter King Midas might have had, imagining every road I traveled would be paved with easy-street gold. I don't know how I came by such delusions except that I hadn't been raised by wolves but by two kind parents, doofus optimists themselves.

For me, then, writing wasn't about onerous struggle; it was about *play,* spinning myself dizzy on purpose, not growing up, doofusness. Whenever I sat down to do it, I felt like I'd dunked my brain into a basin of champagne. No wonder a bland little cucumber didn't mind being plunged into the pickling brine! Writing was a way of being drunk without drinking, of staving off a Miss Clydesdale type of sobriety that, I believed, was the doom awaiting most adults who prioritized respectability above delight. I was a college graduate with a teaching certificate and a husband, but I didn't want to mature into Miss Clydesdale, no matter how respectable she was.

A pal of my mother's, Mrs. Gordon, who was friendly with Mary Jarrell, set up and attended our meeting. Mrs. Gordon looked a little like Jackie Onassis: wide-set eyes, square jaw, cliffs for cheekbones. Unlike many of my mother's brown wren friends, housewifery hadn't dulled Mrs. Gordon to a nub. She wore her light brown hair in a long, saucy pageboy that swung like a hula skirt when she flipped her attentions back and forth to whomever she was talking. She enjoyed talking about the books she was reading. The flirty look in her eyes, her vaguely cynical laugh, her mischievous gift to my mother on her birthday of a bottle of Tanqueray gin made me suspect that despite Mrs. Gordon's country-club outfits, she was kind of an intellectual femme fatale.

Mary Jarrell, a willowy brunette, had a grand, flamboyant smile, one of those gusher smiles a person can't contain. Her hair, dolloped on top of her head, trailed kite tails of flutterments down her neck. A carefree pine needle stuck to the sleeve of her sweater. She gave off the aura of somebody who, despite her literary sophistication, knew the joy of jumping in leaf piles. Her house set back in the woods as if burrowed. Sunlight honeyed over the soft upholstered furniture, and there was the dampish old card-catalog smell of book bindings. An Aubrey Beardsley print hung importantly in the foyer, and shelves towered everywhere, bowed with books, the spines of which looked velvetized from being held. I was a fiend for admiring the Beardsley and leaned forward to glimpse the artist's signature and print run notation. "Oh, it's not *real*," Mary said with a bashful laugh. "It's just a poster." As if to say, I'm not *that* fancy!

Hers was the first writer's house I ever set foot in by invitation. Randall Jarrell had lived there before his death. I'd read his poem "The Death of the Ball Turret Gunner" in high school. To this day, every time I jerk a cart loose from its tangle of nested others and trudge into the dreary milky brightness of a grocery store, I think that his title *A Sad Heart at the Supermarket* says it all.

We discussed two of her late husband's books, *The Bat Poet* and *The Animal Family*. I had recently reread *The Animal Family*—which is about the unlikely coupling of a mermaid and a human and the various animals they adopt and shelter—looking to discover if Jarrell had once used the word *love.* He hadn't. That was the point. There was ample love dramatized in the book without using the word. Mary liked the fact that I'd made the discovery.

That visit with Mary Jarrell was the pinnacle of my success with *The Remarkable Barkable.* It was rejected by ten publishers, and I never sent it out again. Today it's stashed somewhere in my attic where the squirrels who periodically invade that space have probably shredded most of the illustrations to insulate their nests. It was likely a pretty silly book, as most first books are, but for a long time, every time I got a rejection in the mail, I soothed myself by recalling that wonderful summer afternoon spent with two intelligent, book-loving women who had taken such delight in my effort.

Meanwhile, back in the fart world, all nostalgia for my innocence aside, I'm waiting for Miss Clydesdale to report my malfeasance. When the authorities are done with me, just furl me up in a venetian blind and throw me overboard, I'm thinking. I deserve it. I don't belong here. By the time Mr. Snavely arrives at the crime scene, I've stiffened my spine so stoically that somebody could walk the plank on it. How long have I been away from my classroom? Mr. Snavely wants to know. I've been here all along, straightening up the blinds, I tell him. Well, it's almost true. He sniffs around my desk like a bloodhound. What about that peculiar smell? When I explain about the incense, I receive a thistly frown and he warns that it's against fire codes to burn *anything* in a classroom. Why, what if a venetian blind caught fire? What if *all* the blinds caught fire? It would mean the massacre of the venetians. He never mentions the inflammatory music (lucky for me Miss Clydesdale heard *noise* instead), but he stands at the front of the class, his gaze like a minesweep. He's looking for the merest ripple of, say, an arm hair to give somebody away, but for the first time in fart class history, there's not a mutineer in sight.

I find two more rejections in the mailbox when I return home from school that day. One is from Alfred A. Knopf (I was hopeful they'd like the book because their logo is a running dog) and the other is from Scribner's. I picked Scribner's because it was Hemingway's publisher and I'm in a swoon over Hemingway ever since finishing Flaubert. Sad-sack Emma Bovary would have lasted about one minute as a fart teacher at North Forsyth. Hemingway's Jake Barnes is a different story—he suffers well.

I know a few things clearly: I hate teaching art because I'm simply no good at letting it be fart instead; I hate monitoring my hem length and wearing my hair screwed up in a knot like Miss Clydesdale's; I hate going into the teachers' lounge—the choking wall of cigarette smoke, the jellybean colors of Tupperware, the soul-dicing glances and silences you want to kick because the faces making them are so ugly. I've always hated the lounge, but the *next* time I enter, I'll detect the toxic exhaust of Miss Clydesdale's hit-and-run. The gossips will have all been picking at me like buzzards glommed on roadkill.

I know one more thing: tonight, after I file away the newest rejections, carp a little, and snivel out some self-pity, I'm going to tuck into reading more Hemingway and steep myself in bravery a while. Afterward, if I'm not too sleepy, I'll write. I haven't a clue what I'll write, but I know without a doubt that I'll write something.

Five

Empathy in Overdrive

One morning while I'm teaching, I start feeling queasy. I barely make it to the teachers' lounge before I throw up. Afterward, convinced I'm coming down with some crud, I head home. But a strange thing happens as I drive. Mile by mile my spirits lift, along with the debilitating nausea. By the time I arrive at the apartment, I'm feeling as buoyant as a helium balloon let loose from a child's grubby hand into the liberating sky-blue ether.

It's 1974 and my husband and I are living in Chapel Hill where he's enrolled full-time at the University of North Carolina as a doctoral candidate in English literature. To support us, I'm still teaching art, this time at a junior high school in Durham County, a thirty-minute commute from Chapel Hill. There's a gas shortage in America; motorists often wait in long lines at the pumps and prices are high. To conserve energy, daylight savings time is observed nationwide year-round and a 55-mile-per-hour speed limit imposed. The war in Vietnam dwindles, but the number of

war veterans now totals more than six and a half million.
An embittered artist sprays "KILL YES ALL" on Picasso's
famous painting *Guernica* at the Museum of Modern Art
in New York City.

Streaking is the newest major fad on college campuses.
It's skinny-dipping without the water. The University
of Georgia sets a record when more than 1,500 students
simultaneously streak, and streaking marks many cultural
events that year, including the Academy Awards. Novelty
stuntman Philippe Petit walks a high wire strung between
the twin towers of the World Trade Center 1,350 feet above
New York City. A young California heiress, Patty Hearst,
gets abducted by the Symbionese Liberation Army and
held for ransom. Richard Nixon is impeached for his role
in the Watergate scandal and resigns.

I watch Nixon's televised exit, his arms, as flamboyant
as semaphores, waving an indefatigable goodbye to everybody before he boards the helicopter that will transport
him into civilian life, a disgraced president, his face
collapsing like candle tallow, dripping sweat and tears and
phony pluck, his smile transparently sad. I am shocked to
see how vulnerable he looks, how chastened in spite of
his bravado. I will remember him as being green. I don't
mean the sallow tint of green-around-the-gills green that
a sick person turns. He has every right to feel sick. No,
what I'm seeing is the wobbly bright Jell-O see-through
green of a fluoroscope screen: *exposure* green. I can see
every shadowy twitching of Nixon's human bones. I feel
ashamed that we have a ruined X-ray of a president, but
let me be perfectly clear: I feel immensely sorry for the
man, too. In a shockingly visceral way, I can imagine
myself standing in his hard leather, airless tie shoes and
dark, itchy, sweltering socks, imagine how it feels to be
picking from my closet rack the last presidential tie with

which I'll noose my neck for my presidential swan song; I conjure the sound of my aides gently knuckling on my door to tell me it's time for my execution. Blisters of perspiration glob my upper lip; waterfalls of sweat gush from my underarms. Must I wear a coat? It's hotter than Hades. Whenever I cringe over my plight of teaching art to a bunch of subhumans at Carrington Junior High, whenever my assignment feels so bleak that, staring out a classroom window into the parking lot I do this Zen thing of trading places with a rock beside the tire of my car, I tell myself to remember Nixon's humiliation. My ordinary mortal's unhappiness and accountability has got to be peanuts compared to that.

It's my last year in the MFA program at UNC-Greensboro where I've studied fiction writing almost exclusively with Fred Chappell. After Thursday-night workshops, everybody hangs out at the Pickwick, a grimy little bar on Chapman Street near campus. Conversations begun in class tend to deepen at the Pickwick, beer serving as truth serum. One night, Fred's got something he wants to tell me, and he's working up the courage. He has this mannerism, a contortion of facial muscles, kind of like a pitcher's windup, that starts out nonchalant, revs up a ferocious hesitancy, then lets loose a gaze so audacious his face is coming at you faster than a fly ball. "Remember the poems you submitted with your grad school application?" he asks. I nod. Now he's lighting a cigarette, blowing out the match, dragging deep, and exhaling the smoke in a contemplative, dawdling way. Gosh, is he ever a ruminator. "There's one or two decent poems in the batch," he says, sucking the foam off his beer. "The metronome poem's okay. For what it is, you know? But then there's that goofy Gerard Manly Hopkins thing and those sappy beach

THE
RICHARD NIXON
OF POETRY

poems. Anyway," he sighs long and hard then puffs his stalling cigarette, "I sure as hell am glad it turns out you can write fiction, because you ain't no poet, kid." Then, I swear, he chuckles!

Funny thing is, I'm not offended by his remark. He delivers it with such shrugging aplomb that it's as if he thinks he's confirming my own low opinion of my poetry anyway. Of *course* I didn't *really* believe my poems were any good, did I? Surely I could tell that I was dealing in literary betrayal. Did I really want to become the Richard Nixon of poetry? Facing up to my limitations, I can spare the world from all those ghastly poems I might have written, right? Fred unburdens himself from his pronouncements as if they're of no more matter to my self-esteem than rejecting a too-bulky coat in favor of one that's a better fit. Sure, you could say that in one fell swoop of wordage, he's axed half of my writing life, the poetry half. My triumph is that he didn't axe the fiction half as well.

I commute every Thursday night to UNC-Greensboro for the fiction workshop. I carpool with a fellow student, Brock, who also lives in Chapel Hill, is married, and has a young daughter. My husband suspects Brock has the hots for me. It's an accusation, not a compliment. Brock and I share rides because with the gas shortage it would be stupid and wasteful not to. Sure, yeah, *right,* my husband sneers. He's been reading way too much Henry James or something. But I guess if the president of the United States can lie, everybody's suspect.

My school-morning routine continues: I wake up in good spirits, eat breakfast, throw up. I'm not pregnant. I don't have a fever. It's not the flu. Maybe it's just the world we live in—all the lies and tough truths. Nevertheless, I trundle on.

Mr. Bender, the principal of Carrington Junior High, resembles large appliance packaging. He is about the size and shape of a box that a low-end refrigerator would come in. He is just as self-contained, a stiff-shouldered rectangular block of a man, blank features, cardboard-colored complexion. He has very small eyes, galvanized gray, tight lips that mumble. He is never out and about in the hallways, collaring the troublemakers. He sits so heavily implanted behind his desk that you'd need a hand truck to budge him. I'm not aware he has appendages of any sort.

But who really needs a principal? I have learned how to preside over the crude, rude, and disruptive. This is where having an imagination comes in handy. You simply edit bad students out. You reinvent them as something other than human beings: beige and brown flotsam and jetsam bobbing over the art tables, lumpish head-things surfacing here and there, their tentacles curling damply around paint brushes and flopping ineptly around. It helps to think of them as inept rather than incorrigible. Most are drowsing, sulking, blobbing, mouthing, and ruining—not painting. They are models of productivity in its death throes. One day Mr. Bender calls me down to the office to sign some document, and when I return, the creatures have united to dismantle the art tables and throw them out the windows. I gawk in admiration: it's the most creative thing they've ever done.

I am starting to throw up every morning before I go to work. But it's not just work that makes me queasy. Sometimes, even in the blandest of locations, the nonthreatening grocery store for example, my knees spool into syrup. I start identifying with the live lobsters in their tank, grieving for them, and I don't want to be in charge of a basket of groceries any more than a classroom of kids. The thought of going to a party with my husband's English grad student pals disables me with a nausea so profound that sometimes by the time we get there, anxiety has soldered me to the car seat. "You go on in," I tell him. "I'll just sit here and watch the stars come out." I go to one party, where everybody's smoking marijuana, and I niche myself into a corner by the record player turntable. It's a comfort watching the records spinning predictably around and around. The Allman Brothers. Roberta Flack's album, *Killing Me Softly with His Song*. Beverly Sills singing an aria from *Lucia*. Plop, another record drops, and Stevie Wonder belts out something melodious.

"What are you doing all crammed in the corner?" my husband asks, sidling up. "Come join the conversation."

"If I join the conversation, I'll throw up. Maybe the wallpaper's making me dizzy. Does it look like it's moving to you?"

He sighs. "Stop acting weird. It's like you're sitting in some kind of paranoid antisocial trance."

"Listen to them and their self-congratulation," I say, gesturing towards the roomful of cackling students. "Posturing as hip intellectuals. Bragging on all the Joan Didion and Ursula LeGuin and Walker Percy and Joseph Heller and John Barth and Thomas Pynchon they've scarfed down this week when they ought to have been grooving on their Chaucer and *Beowulf*."

My husband's eyes look as red as a werewolf's, and he's three sheets to the wind. Maybe he laughs but probably not. "What's your point?"

"It's all boring as hell," I say. "That's my point."

"It's been said that when something bores you, it's probably boring most deeply." He's *always* lecturing. "You might like some of those books yourself."

"When do I have time to *read* anymore? I'm too busy teaching art to subhumans and puking my guts out. Holy moly, the wallpaper over your left shoulder is killing me. I feel like I'm on a tilt-a-whirl."

"You don't have to talk about books. Talk about other things."

"Well, I've read Milton," I say. "Even excruciating Milton, like *Areopagitica*. Doesn't that count for conversation anymore? Think they could talk about Milton? Shakespeare? We could talk about *real* literature since they're all working on their fancy damn Ph.D. degrees. But *no,* those imposters would rather talk about *Monty Python's Flying Circus* and *Zen and the Art of Motorcycle Maintenance.*"

"You love *Monty Python,*" he reminds me. "Hey, I don't think you should smoke any more pot."

It's Thursday again and I'm riding home late from fiction workshop with Brock, feeling decently mellow after a couple of Pickwick beers. Fred slammed one of my stories tonight, but that's okay. Story-schmory. It was a Flannery O'Connor knockoff about a redneck trucker in the live-haul business who pulls his chicken truck into a gas station that's being robbed. Suddenly there are lots of guns and feathers. During the melee, the trucker unlatches the chicken cages. All the humans end up dead and the birds, free and alive and symbolic as hell. It's a stupid story, I know that *now,* post–public humiliation. What business do I have writing about truckers in the live-haul business anyway? It's because my empathy's in overdrive night and day. It all started with Nixon. Sometimes, driving behind a chicken-loaded truck on my commute to Carrington Junior High, I can identify so completely with the chickens mashed against the bars of their cages, terrified by the speed, the blast of wind, the angry-smelling diesel fumes, that my hands turn into chicken feet gripping the steering wheel. I can imagine the sort of panic that turns a chicken's brain to slosh. If I were one of them, I'd be a puddle of soup by the time the truck hauling me pulled up to the slaughterhouse.

At the end of workshop discussion, Fred sat glaring at the story. He struck a match to light his cigarette, but he held it so long, watching the flame, that I thought he was going to torch the manuscript. "Naw," he says finally. "I don't believe a word. This here, darlin', is Andy Griffith meets Superfly."

Brock's at the wheel tonight and, gosh, it feels relaxing to simply be the passenger. Last week I drove us in the rain and did a hit-and-run on a opossum that's going to take me months to get over. I much prefer being the passenger. Sometimes when I'm the driver, I get the nausea in anticipation of something going wrong. I'm telling Brock about Milton's theological radicalism. Well, somebody's got to do it. The guy's never even read *Paradise Lost.* Back in college, I say, I took my textbook and flipped through all the pictures of Milton as a young man and inked in Beatles-style hair and Picadilly Circus collars. I updated him out of respect because he was such a revolutionary.

Brock likes hearing about Milton. He's not a know-it-all like *some* people I could name. He's another writer suffering from low self-esteem just like me, and I feel very tender towards him all of a sudden.

We exit I-40 onto Highway 86, a curvy back road that winds us in a southerly direction, away from Hillsborough towards Chapel Hill. When we cross the railroad tracks near the barbecue joint, Brock jams on brakes and pulls over.

"What's the matter?" I ask, peering out my window, looking for another creamed opossum.

"The stars are the matter," he says in a soft, admiring voice. "Cassiopeia. Orion's belt. But I don't see them. They're not where they're supposed to be."

Uh-oh. Is my husband right about Brock after all? Here we are, pulled over in the middle of nowhere to *stargaze*? What have I summoned, feeling tender towards Brock? He's pointing skyward, but I don't see a thing except a milky smear of light, and my naïveté seems more unfathomable than all the galaxies churning above. I remember when foolishness used to make me feel as sparkly as a dare. Now all my moving parts have suddenly ground to a halt.

"Guess I'm still a little drunk" is all he says. "Would you mind driving the rest of the way to your house?" Me and my imagination.

I'm throwing up like crazy every morning now. I'm a wraith of my former lanky self, having lost twenty pounds. I weigh less than I did in junior high school, and I was so skinny then I was practically invisible. Every evening when I come home from teaching, I'm close to tears. Plus I've started doing this sicko empathy number on myself in the mornings when I turn on the *Today* show. I imagine I'm whatever guest Barbara Walters is interviewing, doesn't matter who. Imagining that millions of people are watching me, I can make myself turn quadriplegic with stage fright. I've got the sprung throat feeling, dried up salivary glands, nausea rising from my gut as heavy as a levitating anvil. Then, the instant Barbara asks a question, I've got the brain drainage. Doesn't matter what the question is. It can be as simple as "What's your name?" My brain cells scatter like a ream of blank paper dropped into a hurricane.

"Turn off the television. You're going to be late for school," my husband says.

"I've got to finish the interview," I say. It feels crucial to find this stuff out sooner rather than later: that I turn to jelly in the spotlight; that I'm not solid enough to hold up under scrutiny of any kind; I'm not bold enough at art, writing, teaching, being a wife, being *me*. Instead, I'm out there glomming on to everyone's identity but my own. I'm just this big amorphous squish. Is this what writers mean when they talk about "finding a voice?" That, first, you have to sink as low as an amoeba?

My husband gives me a mandate. "You're quitting your teaching job."

"I am?"

"It's making you crazy. You're going to that damn school in the morning and you're giving Mr. Block your notice."

"His name is Mr. Bender."

"If you can't come home this afternoon and tell me you've given him two weeks' notice, I'll call him myself."

"How are we going to pay our bills?"

"You'll find another job."

That day, when I blab my resignation spiel, I see for the first time that Mr. Bender has arms and legs. The moment the announcement leaves my mouth, he springs from his chair and lunges across the desk. He has hands, too, because he grabs me by my shoulders. "Take two weeks of *paid* leave and think about it," he beseeches. "I beg you not to quit."

"Mr. Bender, I'm miserable here," I tell him. "This school makes me throw up. I've got some weird kind of psychological allergy to it all."

"I know it's bad here," he says. "I know." He's still got my shoulders in a vicelike grip. There's spittle in the corners of his mouth. His rocky face has pinkened with exertion. "Think about it a while before you do something so drastic as to terminate your employment. That's all I'm asking. Don't be rash."

"I *have* been thinking."

"Think *more.*" His gray eyes are foil-shiny and without pupils, like BBs.

"I'm sorry, Mr. Bender, but I've made up my mind."

"UN-make it!" he cries.

I get this terrible feeling that any second he's going to start sniveling. He's going to break down and fall to his knees in a wobbly Jell-O heap of see-through Nixon. Oh, *please* go back to being dull, calm refrigerator packaging, I'm thinking. *Please.* For me, it all started with Nixon: the authorities of the world, the people you're supposed to be able to count on as guides and leaders, bailing. My generation is the one that came up with the mantra, "Don't trust anybody over thirty." And so it's happening. Freaky Mr. Bender is just another monster we've created.

"So did you give your notice today?" my husband asks when I return home.

"I don't know."

"What do you mean you don't know? Either you did or you didn't."

"It's lots more complicated than that," I say. "I feel really really really *really* sorry for Mr. Bender."

But I do quit the teaching job, and I start commuting via Trailways bus to Greensboro, three days a week, where I work oiling and testing and packing scissors for my father-in-law's company. The good news is that Ernestine, who sits beside me at the inspection table, is permitted to watch her little portable TV while she eats lunch, and, between her soaps, there's usually a newsbreak to update America on Patty Hearst. Her kidnappers' ransom demand is for two million dollars' worth of food for the poor and the disenfranchised. That's before Patty falls in love with one of the kidnappers and becomes an outlaw herself. Eventually a bank camera will photograph her wearing a black beret and cradling a weapon.

After the newsbreak, I go back to my pile of scissors. I test their cutting quality on a strip of muslin. Ernestine brags that when she gently squeezes the open scissors shut, she can *hear* the burrs on their blades. Burrs cause the scissors to snag. Her ability to hear burrs makes her something of a scissors savant in my father-in-law's eyes.

Because he thinks scissors are an art form, we're expected to handle them as if they're museum-quality artifacts. (Scissors, along with the safety pin, were actually invented by the ancients.) But my grip is slippery and weak; my dedication, nil. Plus I'm always dropping the product. My father-in-law can hear me drop a pair of scissors from his office at the far end of the building. To his ears, it's an auditory event as politically loaded as burning the flag. It's all about my generation's slipshod concentration, a work ethic subverted by too much navel-gazing. I can't hear burrs on the blades, but I can hear my father-in-law's blood boiling. Eight hours a day, thirty minutes off for lunch, I sit beside Ernestine, testing scissors, dropping them, adjusting the torque of their screws, then oiling each pair, slipping them into little prophylactic papooses that we tuck into gift boxes as plush as bassinettes.

Meanwhile, Patty's blindfold has been taken off, she's out of her closet and on the lam, making love to revolutionaries and shooting up banks. Now I ask you: between Patty and me, whose life is the stuff that fires the imagination? Who's piling up the best experiences for writer fodder?

"So what I'm hearing is that you would rather be taken hostage by the lunatic fringe than to work at a scissors factory? Would that be your 'child self' or your 'adult self' speaking? And thank you for sharing," Ken says. He's a Chapel Hill psychologist with a massive practice—legions of English graduate students flock to his office, which is how I find out about him. Since we have no health insurance, I've joined Ken's "low-fee" group that meets for an hour a week at the bargain-basement rate of five dollars a pop. Ken facilitates a brand of group therapy called transactional analysis. As best as I can determine, it's all about coaxing the patient to solve his or her own problems. Ken's role isn't to inform or advise. It's to prod in a non-judgmental way, without a hint of emotional investment in my answer. His eyes don't blink. The expression on his face is as impassive as a lizard's.

There are a half dozen folks in our low-fee group, counting Ken. He participates as both leader and member. He's recently remarried, and his new wife wants to have a baby, but Ken doesn't. Another guy—Brad, mid-thirties, sandy-colored beard, mild eyes—confesses that he's tormented about whether to leave his wife. He simply doesn't love her anymore—but is that enough reason to leave? Fern and Alex are a couple striving not to murder one another in cold blood. They consciously pick their worst fights in public places so that if things get out of hand, there'll be plenty of people around to stop them from going too far. There's a young woman named Valerie whose mother is a lunatic. Me, I've got the nausea.

"When I think about my life, I feel like throwing up. When I think about Patty's, I don't," I tell the group.

"I hear you," Ken says. "Go with that."

"Go where?"

"Explore that thought. What do you think it *means?*"

"You're the psychologist. You tell me."

"I appreciate your frustration, and thank you for sharing it with the group."

The trouble with transactional analysis is that it's like a guessing game. It seems as if the person with the psychology degree could move us all along more quickly to resolving our questions and dilemmas, but he won't. Transactional analysis presumes that you are the expert on yourself. But if I'm such an expert on myself, why can't I figure out a way to stop feeling nauseated? Ken would say, if he were allowed to speak normally, that I can't figure out how to stop the nausea because I don't yet know I'm an expert on myself. But I have to be the one to arrive at that insight, not Ken. Right now I am an expert in denial.

"Do you think I'm more of a hostage than Patty?"

"A hostage to whom?" Ken asks.

"I'm being ridiculous. Forget it. I'm not a hostage."

"You aren't?"

"You tell *me*!"

"I hear you. Thank you for sharing. We need to move on to Fern and Alex."

What probably annoys me the most about transactional analysis is the language, the dim-witted call-and-response politeness of it all. It's driving me nuts.

"Ken," I say, "I hate the formulaic way we talk in this group. *Why* do we have to talk this way?"

"What way?"

"LIKE BABBLING BABY IDIOT ROBOTS!"

"I hear you. Good. It's perfectly okay to own that feeling."

"I'm a writer," I say. "Words matter to me. The uniqueness of individual expression matters."

"I hear you."

"OF COURSE YOU HEAR ME. I'M SITTING THREE FEET FROM YOU, KEN!"

"Thank you for expressing yourself so forthrightly and clearly," Ken says. "You might want to ask yourself if you express yourself as clearly and forthrightly to people *outside* our therapy group. That's merely a suggestion for further thought. I'm not telling you what to do."

I can think of few writers worth the paper their books are printed on who haven't paid their waylaying troublesome dues. D. H. Lawrence taught school as unhappily as I. Worse, when he and his wife, Frieda, were living hand to mouth, he'd sit writing at the kitchen table, and they'd get into such violent fights that she'd bang him in the head with a frying pan; Faulkner worked long, dulling hours in a factory where he claimed to have written *As I Lay Dying* in six weeks despite a roaring backdrop of machinery; Hemingway was an ambulance driver in World War I and suffered wounds; Gertrude Stein, who quit medical school and lived in Paris as an expatriate, couldn't find a publisher until she was well into middle age. Elizabeth Barrett Browning was a bedridden invalid for much of her literary life. Was it from nausea?

It's not that writers, no matter their burdens, go stumbling forth expecting that their luck will change either. They just go stumbling forth. The stumbling a writer does in life probably matters more than any success, because it's the stumbling that tests one's capacity for resilience. You can't endure as a writer without it any more than you can without a fair measure of dumb luck. Novelist Mary Lee Settle has written that more than will and talent, it takes *empathy* to be a good writer. I would add that it takes at least as much resilience, which arises from a peculiar, dogged faith in your own abstract uncertainties to pan out, to lead *somewhere* other than to the edge of a high cliff. Occasionally resilience and self-delusion are one and the same, but writers are often incapable of making a distinction.

Sometime during 1974, I read in the paper that a young woman poet living near Tinker Creek in rural Virginia has won the Pulitzer Prize for nonfiction. Her name is Annie Dillard and she is only a couple of years older than me. She's married to the writer Richard Dillard, who teaches at Hollins College and whose work I have read and admired. Annie Dillard's lyrical meditation on the natural world she meticulously observed near her home began as a private journal and ended up a prize-winning book.

I imagine, first, her life. And then her joy. I'm as good as *there,* in the kitchen with young Annie. She's cooking supper one ordinary afternoon when the phone rings with the news. She's not thinking about the things she has written about in *Pilgrim at Tinker Creek.* Not the courtship of the praying mantises, the way the female bites off the head of her male partner *before* sex or about spiders so big and powerful they trap and eat hummingbirds. Not about sycamore trees or muskrats or the tragic Polyphemus moth. I envision her intent on measuring ingredients, making a pot of soup I can almost smell. Because one thing I know from reading *Tinker Creek* is that Annie Dillard knows how to fiercely inhabit the moment. I am convinced that she extracts more of life's juices from an hour than some people extract from decades. Her face is moist from leaning into the soup pot's steam to taste and season the broth. She cocks her head as if to *listen* to the taste. She wants to add more pepper. She's got her long blonde hair in braids. She's barefooted, like a hillbilly, and wearing old jeans with holes in the knees through which her kneecaps poke. I wouldn't be a bit surprised to see her stir the soup with her toe, because, like a butterfly, she can probably *taste* with her feet. She lopes towards the ringing phone as she chews nonchalantly on a carrot stick. She's humming some off-key nontune like a happy carpenter. This is the prize-winning writer in private whose book was conceived in privacy as something initially for *her* sake, not anybody else's. She answers the phone blankly, not expecting anything, perhaps distracted from the task by the radiant tang of the carrot she's eating, perhaps, staring at a distant wall, dimly aware of the *muscae volitantes* she's written about, those curly, moving amoebic spots you sometimes see as you gaze into thin air. Her mouth's full of carrot when she finds out, and the *muscae volitantes* turn into pinwheeling stars. That's how I imagine it: the way it would happen to me, smack-dab in the thick of everything else.

I've published a mere three stories at the time Annie Dillard wins the Pulitzer Prize. But nothing seems to be stopping me from writing more. Not Richard Nixon or Mr. Bender or transactional analysis or the drabbest toil in the scissors factory. Not the nausea either. It occurs to me that the one place I am blissfully free of nausea is at my writing desk.

"I do what I normally do when I get good news: I jump up and down on the bed."

Six

Virginia Woolf on a Motorcycle

Down South, in 1975, feminism is still pretty much a gleam in the rabble-rouser's eye, and elsewhere, women are making as much hair-raising as consciousness-raising news: Patty Hearst finally gets arrested by the FBI; best-selling fiction includes Judith Rossner's *Looking for Mister Goodbar* about a woman who picks a psycho for a boyfriend; Lynette "Squeaky" Fromme, a former Manson family member, gets arrested for aiming a gun at President Ford. Despite its being International Women's Year, efforts to pass state-level equal rights amendments in New York and New Jersey fail. Pop singers the Captain and Tennille appear on some TV show, decked out like a corny nautical version of Sonny and Cher. Will somebody please tell me why *he* gets to be captain when *she's* the one with the talent?

But there's some good news for women, too: Harvard finally opens its doors to as many qualified women as men applicants. Plus it's no longer okay to say "fireman" or "chairman." One is encouraged to substitute the gender-neutral term *person,* as in "personhole" rather than manhole, even though "personhole" sounds obscene.

In the spirit of upheaval, I've recently published in the *Carolina Quarterly* a bizarre, quasi-feminist story, "Variations on a Scream," that has led to my winning a scholarship to the venerable Bread Loaf Writers' Conference in August. "Variations on a Scream" (which I refer to as my "pervert story") is an assemblage of tongue-in-cheek vignettes. The men in the story are wolves, molesters, opportunists, and freaks. The women are all as naïve as Brownie Scouts. Never mind that my graduate school mentor, Fred Chappell, tells me ruefully that "Variations on a Scream" is the silliest story I ever wrote; it's oddly au courant.

I meet Max Steele, the director of UNC's creative writing program, at the English department's annual sherry party, and he tells me that he read the story in the *Quarterly* and liked it, although he doesn't know what to make of it. Literary flattery—even the faintest whiff of it—is hallucinogenic. My mind goes wild with it. I can believe what I want to believe. So what if he doesn't understand the story? I don't quite understand it myself. But didn't Flannery O'Connor claim that the best stories resist paraphrase? Liking without understanding is the way I often feel when I parse a verse of T. S. Eliot or listen to Bartók or peer into the frenzied undertow of a de Kooning painting.

Of course at this particular party I've had more than my quota of sherry. Saucing ourselves is the only way most of us minor characters—the grad students and their spouses—work up the courage to have conversations with some of the professorial potentates oscillating around the banquet table. Faculty wives with cloudy hairdos float among us as benign as angels. *Why* do we *do* this every year? they're probably asking themselves. Oh, yes, of course. Because without us there would be *only* sherry. No deviled eggs and ham biscuits and brownies and watermelon pickles and fried chicken and seven-layer salad or pound cake. Nobody would *eat* if it weren't for us. All the students would go home drunk *and* hungry! Anyway, Max's acknowledging that he read my story and puzzled its lacunae with no dire results makes my insides hum long after the sherry wears off.

Midsummer, I run into him again at the Big Star grocery store in Chapel Hill. I'm in Produce. The fluorescent lights jitter brightly; the linoleum bangs with shine. The vegetables—the bell peppers look especially jaunty—surround us with the kicky colors of a chorus line. Or maybe I feel like dancing myself because Max remembers me from the sherry party, salutes, and steers his cart to where I'm picking through a bin of potatoes. But the closer he comes, the more I start feeling like a tuber myself, going round-shouldered with a brown, dusty shyness. Should I call him Max or Mr. Steele? Did he like my story or didn't he? It didn't make sense to him, but it was worth puzzling over—right? He flattered me into thinking it was deep, not silly. Or I flattered myself into thinking that.

Meeting an immortal in the plain old grocery store makes for a kind of awkward intimacy. We're leaning over mundane shopping baskets that expose and demystify our inner tickings the way purses and closets do. A basket of groceries is an X-ray of one's persnicketies and enfeeblements. Thank god I don't have a box of tampons in mine. I cast a discreet glance at Max's loot, hoping to see some humanizing oddity that will undermine the intimidating myth of him I've let build since the sherry gala. A box of Ex-Lax would do the trick, but his basket is empty, as filled with possibility as a blank page in a *Ding Dong School Book.*

He's got an aura, a mischievous pompousness, the literary luster of having published stories in the *New Yorker* and served as an editor of the *Paris Review*. He's pals with people like George Plimpton, Carolyn Kizer, and Alice Adams. He has the erect, confident posture of somebody wearing epaulets. He's not wearing epaulets, of course; he's wearing a summery seersucker suit with a light blue stripe. The blue matches the color of his eyes.

A tall, ruddy, stylish man, about fifty, with a shock of hair that glints yellowish silver in the fluorescence, Max is handsome in a Spencer Tracy sort of way. He darts at me sideways (he's fond of hit-and-run conversations): "I've been thinking some more about your story in the *Quarterly*," he says. "Sometimes the writing's a little like Virginia Woolf on a motorcycle."

Is this good or bad? I'm trying to picture Virginia Woolf on a motorcycle. What kind of motorcycle? Is she straddling it, or is she tucked into a sidecar?

"Think you'd like to teach some writing classes at UNC in the fall?"

It happens that fast. My brain goes from zero to a hundred miles an hour—Virginia Woolf on a *runaway* motorcycle. I'm ascending from probable potato to possible professor, standing right there in Produce at the Big Star. Such art-affirming, life-changing solicitations are not supposed to happen so offhandedly! I've only published five stories in small-circulation literary magazines. I don't have a doctoral degree. Is this a joke? Before I can stutter forth any semblance of response, he disengages from further conversation as if he suspects the fruits and vegetables of eavesdropping. "I'll call you," he says, glancing suspiciously at the potatoes.

"Why did Mr. and Mrs. Potatohead refuse to let their daughter date Walter Cronkite?" he asks. "Because he was a common tater," he answers himself, keeping a poker face. Then he lurches away, making a beeline towards a pyramid of tomatoes. I don't see him again until the checkout line, where he pays cash for a single magnificent tomato, glides, as if on casters, through the Big Star doors into the July-baked parking lot, and vaporizes like a genie.

Max calls, and we have a formal meeting in his office on campus before he escorts me downstairs to meet the chairperson of the English department, Bill Harmon. Bill's a tall, lanky poet-scholar with an expression on his face like a flashbulb's just gone off. His bespectacled eyes seem to bulge because of all the brains packed in behind them. The grad students say that Bill's not only hip and witty, he's scary smart, with a mind as colorful and busily alive as a coral reef. "Did you hear that the guy who wrote 'The Hokey Pokey' just died at ninety-two?" Max calls to Bill at the threshold of his office.

"The rough part's what happened at the funeral," Bill says. "They had trouble keeping his body in the casket. They stuck his right foot in, he stuck his right foot out . . . well, you probably know the rest."

Lord, this is the sort of company I'm going to be keeping if I get this job. Jokesters all around. I can't remember jokes anybody tells me, except the Little Moron series that I learned in first grade.

Max introduces me to Bill, and I reach out to shake hands. As we're about to make contact, Bill swiftly retracts the hand he's extended, waggles it as if it's on fire, and yelps. "You *don't* want to touch it! It's not poisonous, but it's ugly!"

I jump back in case he's holding a spider. Max is laughing.

"It's either eczema or leprosy," Bill says, fanning his fingers and rotating the hand so that I can see its inflammation. "Itches like hell. Sorry, didn't mean to shock you."

"You did so," Max says. "It was a test."

"Still think you'd like to teach here?" Bill asks.

I nod like a bobblehead.

"Good," he says, "you're hired." It is really that easy.

"I want you to remember something," Max says to me as we're ambling down the corridor afterward. "We're not just hiring you to teach; we're hiring you to write. Don't forget about the writing."

"I get withdrawal symptoms when I don't write," I assure him. "I can't stop myself."

"Yes," he agrees, "there's only one thing harder than being a writer. It's stopping being a writer once you've decided you are one."

I go home from the interview and the glorious job offer and do what I normally do when I get good news: I jump up and down on the bed. I jumped up and down on the bed in 1973 when an editor from the *Carolina Quarterly* called to tell me I'd won second prize in their young writers' contest for my story "Gift." I jumped up and down on the bed in 1974 when the *North American Review* bought my novella "No News."

We're living in a dampish basement apartment on Burlage Circle, about a mile downhill from campus. The ceiling's low and covered in acoustical tiles. When I jump up and down on the bed this time, I conk the crown of my head. The blow to the ceiling unsettles the large extended family of millipedes that live behind the tiles, and they start dropping and scattering in all directions, wiggly beige raindrops with fringe. I don't care. I keep jumping and dancing and singing in the rain of them.

When my husband comes home from the library, I haven't

settled down yet. What's this new feeling? *Legitimacy. Validation.* I've been hired to teach writing because I'm a *writer.* People besides my immediate family *believe*!

"I thought you were going to make moussaka for supper," he says, sniffing the dank, flavorless basement air.

"I'm too excited to cook."

"Well, it *is* good news," he concedes, "although teaching two courses isn't going to leave you much time for your own work."

"Compared to teaching public school art seven hours a day, five days a week? Compared to the mind-deadening days of packing scissors on an assembly line? Are you kidding me?"

"You'll see," he says.

"Anyway, it's not about having more or less time, it's about finally getting to use my brain."

"What brain? Just kidding."

Later that night we're finishing a waylaid supper of Chinese takeout, and he's sulking because he picked the dud fortune cookie with the scrambled platitude: "'Man who laughs last, laughs least.'"

"Let's see what yours says." He breaks open my cookie and unfurls the fortune. "'Your creativity will bring you big rewards.' Damn," he says.

Well, he has every right to be jealous. He's been steeping his brain in canonical literature for years now, getting word-drunk on everybody from Henry Fielding to Saul Bellow, wading eyebrow-deep in literary minutiae, teaching freshman composition classes, and scuttling the halls of academe as an awed and supplicant grub among the professorial Monarchs.

I come breezing in with my welterweight MFA degree and a handful of published short stories and presto-chango,

I get to be a university professor overnight. Mine's a fake poetic license, that's what he's thinking. I can tell by the sniggering expression on which he's slapped a weak restraining order.

"Did you ever finish *Moby-Dick*?" he asks out of the blue.

"Nope. Please don't tattle on me to Max or Professor Harmon."

"Did you ever finish *Absalom, Absalom*?"

"I have thirty-five pages left," I confess.

"That was months ago. You're not going to finish it, are you? How can you be thirty-five pages away from the end of such a significant book and not finish?"

"It got a little oppressive, to tell you the truth. But the part about the French architect escaping through the trees like a squirrel is pure genius."

"What about that Conrad story I gave you to read, 'Outpost of Progress?'"

"I read it."

"And what did you think?"

"Well, it might have gone faster if I'd had a machete handy. Those pages are pretty thick with jungle."

"How can you make jokes?"

"I can't make jokes. I'm terrible at jokes."

He sits there looking morose, shredding his nonfortune. "You're going to get busted flat," he says. "When some student wants to discuss narrative tension in *Moby-Dick*, what will you say if you haven't read the damn thing?"

"I'll say I haven't read the damn thing."

"Oh, brother."

"And then I'll try to explain why. That might be tricky. But I'll talk about something I *have* read: George Garrett's 'Texarkana Was a Crazy Town,' or R. H. W. Dillard's 'The Adventures of the Butterfat Boy,' or this terrific story

I read in the *Atlantic Monthly* not long ago. I told you about it, a comic little tour de force about found art called 'Seven Details the Major Critic of the Show Thought Over-explicit.' It's by an unknown writer named Allan Gurganus. Nobody's ever heard of him, but that doesn't mean he's not worth reading."

All of a sudden being invited to teach creative writing doesn't seem like such a larky bargain. You have to know stuff in order to teach. And what do I really *know* except my unabashed enthusiasm for certain stories and books? They probably don't even come close to being the *right* stories and books, the *approved* ones that land on a proper syllabus.

I've tried to keep up with my husband's reading assignments and earn the shadow Ph.D., but I've given up on too many books to count. Or I've ingested them like doses of medicine, curling my toes inside my shoes, pinching my eyes shut in order to swallow them not whole hog but in bitter increments. I can't read as much Gertrude Stein as is requested of me. I plow through Henry James's *Wings of the Dove*, just barely, and lots of Walker Percy leaves me cold. Ditto Virginia Woolf. O'Connor's *The Violent Bear It Away* seems so much weaker and drawling than her stories. I hunker down with *Moby-Dick* for the umpteenth try. Nothing, except the sensation of drowning.

But the fiction I *do* love accumulates, radiant proof against an intellectual midnight: all of D. H. Lawrence, all of Hemingway, much of John Updike, Ralph Ellison's *Invisible Man*, Faulkner's *As I Lay Dying*, his bizarre un-Faulknerian *Wild Palms* (I loved it), *Light in August* (oh, my, the best book in the world), Fitzgerald's *Tender Is the Night*, Fitzgerald's stories, Cheever's, Peter Taylor's, Salinger's, Chekhov's, Katherine Mansfield's, Katherine

Anne Porter's, Dorothy Parker's, Elizabeth Spencer's, Joyce's *Dubliners* and *A Portrait of the Artist as a Young Man*, more stories by James Baldwin, John Steinbeck, Stanley Elkin, Richard Brautigan, Thomas Mann, Kafka, Isak Dinesen, and Poe. I love Eudora Welty's work so much that I intend to memorize it. I discover Sylvia Plath, Jean Stafford, Rebecca West. I gobble Anne Sexton's poetry and don't care if she's crazy. I read new poems by Fred Chappell or Robert Watson and I think I'm going to burst into flames. I read Willa Cather's *My Antonia,* Turgenev's *Fathers and Sons,* Dreiser's *An American Tragedy,* Somerset Maugham, Graham Greene, Camus. I read Daphne Athas's *Entering Ephesus* and believe I've transcended to the penultimate. Same with William Price Fox's *Ruby Red.* So it's not that I'm a total dullard. I just know what I like better than I know why I don't like what I don't like. How many books would a writer chuck if a writer could chuck books?

But I worry. What if a student asks me about existentialism when we read Sartre's "The Wall" or O'Connor's "A Good Man Is Hard to Find"? What *is* existentialism? I mean *indisputably*? I ask my neighbor Lee Smith, who has published three novels, if she feels a lapse in her education. She's got all kinds of books stacked like wobbly chimneys throughout her house. On the top of one pile I spot *Fear of Flying;* on another, *Watership Down.* "Proust," she says. "I haven't read Proust, and I feel guilty as hell. But I *will* read him. I'm getting there."

I begin to look forward to the Bread Loaf Writers' Conference like a pilgrim preparing for Mecca. Surely I'll learn how to teach creative writing if I pay close attention to the lectures and readings and take a ton of notes. Meanwhile, my husband shoves a bunch of books at me: Philip Stevick's *Theory of the Novel,* Wayne C. Booth's *The Rhetoric of Fiction,* Northrop Frye's *Anatomy of Criticism.*

How can I be such a literary dumbass? I have an MFA degree, and yet I can't readily define the types of irony listed in Thrall, Hibbard, and Holman's *Handbook to Literature.* Isn't irony kind of basic to the creation of all art? How can I have come so far yet have so much further to go in order to pass muster? What *is* muster? My ignorance begets more ignorance.

I am working on a new story I'm calling "Feats" that begins with a couple conceiving a child during a tandem parachute jump. In my diary I note that "I'm at page 25, and the characters all seem to be screaming at me: 'Well, you've gotten us up to this point—*now* what are you going to do to get us out of this mess?" I just can't seem to wrap the thing up. Writing used to be as easy as zooming down a waxed sliding board—until Max Steele told me I *had* to.

I bang my head intermittently against the desk. Two gadfly muses perch on my shoulders, disguising their ordinarily gauzy little fairy freefall selves as taskmasters: Max Steele and Fred Chappell. The Max muse says, "We hired you to write, so write." The Fred muse says, "This story is even sillier than your pervert story." The Max muse is dapper with blue-striped seersucker wings; the Fred muse is a scowly, chain-smoking hoodlum, wearing a windbreaker with the collar turned up.

"You've got two fiends jumping out of a plane and having sex on the way down in your *opening* paragraph," the Fred muse laments, unable to hide his dismay. "First of all, what can you possibly write after such a shocker that won't disappoint the reader, that lives up to this contract?"

"What contract?"

"The contract the writer makes with the reader at the beginning of every story that promises things will only get *more* dazzling and go someplace *clear.*"

"They will?"

"They should," he says. "A writer I know wrote a novel that has, in the first chapter, a jilted fat girl taking a knife and carving the initials of some unrequited hearththrob into her *forehead.*"

"Ouch," the Max muse chimes in. "Then what happens?"

"That's the problem," the Fred muse says. "The reader keeps waiting for something that bold to come along again, but it never does. That's how the book should have *ended.*"

"All stories end up being about *how* they were written," the Max muse tells me. "Look what you titled your story before you've even ended it. You called it 'Feats' right from the start, as if you expected trouble."

"What do you think Max meant when he said my writing reminded him of Virginia Woolf on a motorcycle?" I ask my husband. "Be honest."

He lifts his head from one of Will Durant's tomes—he's been reading about the ancient Egyptians, his eyes ablaze with their lore. "Listen to what this writer wrote in 2100 B.C." he says. "'Everything worth saying has already been said; everything worth writing has already been written.'"

Two days before I leave for the Bread Loaf Writers' Conference near Middlebury, Vermont, I tweak the latest lackluster draft of "Feats," retype it, and write the obligatory analysis that I'm expected to attach to the manuscript. It's a kind of cheat sheet for the perplexed reader—whichever faculty member gets assigned a private consultation with me about my story. I have no inkling how to describe the story except as a pile of clever nonsense. I suspect that the characters are cartoons, but I'm hoping my reader will convince me otherwise. "A feat in itself to end this story well," I conclude in my diary. "There's too much goofiness. It needs a slam-bang of an ending, but . . . last night I dreamed I gave up writing altogether. It once sounded so good to me to 'set up shop as the Farmer Poet.' But 'You forget the Hawk / The Hawk comes down like lightning / He eats chickens up / You're left being merely the Poet, talking shop.'" I am quoting Fred Chappell's poem "Gold and Mean," from his first collection, *The World between the Eyes*. In one form or another, the Fred muse is always with me.

I arrive at Bread Loaf painfully aware that preparing one's mind for the challenges of writing is never the same thing as actually sitting down to write. So what do I expect to glean from my sojourn? Reassurance that the Hawk of self-doubt isn't going to pick this chicken off. If I can't write worth a toot, how can I expect to teach writing? Oh, for some wise, objective evaluator's encouragement to keep doing what I both love and suffer for and can't seem to stop doing, for better or worse, this rowdy Punch and Judy partnering of self and art. But what if every writer is dated for freshness and my date has expired?

It's a strange place, Bread Loaf: a camp for adults, beautiful and heartless—a sloping, pastoral campus nestled amid the Green Mountains and filled with rustic half-timbered buildings, cabins, barns, and Adirondack chairs. Lots of writers posing like significant lawn ornaments, lots of worshipful disciples, lots of pretense, hauteur, and high jinks. It's mid-August, but already the surrounding woods flicker with torchy fall colors. The fragrance of wood smoke clings to the air. Apple trees genuflect with offerings of ripe fruit. I pick and eat an apple from a tree that Robert Frost supposedly planted. There's a birch bark chair in one of the assembly halls folks say he sat in. I find the chair and wallow in it a long, meditative time, hoping to feel the vibes. The days are bright and warm, spangled with butterflies. But at night you can see your breath; it's jacket weather, the wind hoots down from the hills, the camp quiets into scuttlings and whispers, and the black sky pings with stars.

We are three hundred neurotic writer people crammed on a mountaintop at an isolated settlement with a tiny, half-baked post office, three pay phones, and a bus stop connecting us to the outside world. There is an older couple who go everywhere dressed like twins; there is a man who braids his long beard in a pigtail. The big shots stand around in the evening, drinking their Bloody Marys and lionizing one another. Hilma Wolitzer, Francine Prose, Lore Segal, and Nancy Willard are friendly. Nancy Willard has a face like a sunflower and radiant Lady Godiva hair streaming down her back. She looks like she knows how to fly. She wears gauzy dresses and shoes as dainty as leaves. She hasn't yet written *A Visit to William Blake's Inn,* which I will one day read to my children, but some sense of a wavelength between us makes me wish mightily that she were my reader. Instead, I've been assigned a writer named Frank Elliot whose story "In Chibobo Land"—a kind of nutshell version of Bellow's *Henderson the Rain King*—I've read in an anthology. Frank is suspicious of my Southern accent. I can tell right away he thinks I'm a hick by the fact that he doesn't rise from his chair to greet me when I enter his lodgings to have my private conference. He probably thinks manners are wasted on hicks.

He's middle-aged, grayish, lean but barrel-chested, with a face like a wolfhound. He's slouched in his chair, looking sleepy. "So," he says, ruffling the pages of my manuscript, "what's this story about? What should I get from it?"

I shrug. "Whatever you get from it, I guess." I start retracting myself like a slimy little snail's foot.

"What were you trying to prove or clarify or question about life as we humans know it?"

"I thought I knew," I say softly, "but by the time I got to the end, I didn't."

"I thought so," he says, a little too triumphantly.

"I was hoping you'd tell me that the story makes more sense than I think."

"It doesn't. Sorry to disappoint you." He's not sorry one bit.

I disappear myself into such a tiny smear of mortified nothingness that he's not even looking at me anymore, just at the manuscript. He's talking to the manuscript as if he's in the room alone with it, or wishes that he were, so that he could just toss it and be done with the folderol of this tutorial. The way he's glaring at the pages, the story appears to have all the lucidity of a bucket of tar.

"Can it be fixed?" I ask.

"About as easily as world hunger. Listen, Mary Jane," he says, "first thing a writer's got to know is what his story's about. He can't expect other people to know if he doesn't. He can't fix what's broken until he knows what's broken. And he can't know what's broken if he can't tell broken from fixed."

I don't know whether it's the Hawk or existentialism that grabs hold of me. "*She*," I say.

"I beg your pardon?"

"*She's* got to know what *her* story's about. Sir."

I slouch around for a few days, avoiding Frank Elliot's tendency to look right through me as if I'm a windowpane with no vista beyond. Then—maybe it's the fool's gold weather or the twilight Bloody Marys—I rally. After all, I'm here to glean wisdom, not compliments, aren't I? I attend a wonderful lecture by the novelist John Gardner. The room is so packed that Gardner asks somebody to open the window because he feels faint. Another night, a writer nobody much has heard of reads the dazzling opening chapter for his book-in-progress, *The World According to Garp*. Younger Bread Loaf scholarship and fellowship awardees give readings, among them a boyish, aw-shucks Tim O'Brien who everybody's comparing to Hemingway, and the poet Tess Gallagher, solemn as an asparagus. Somebody encourages me to read a portion of "Variations on a Scream," and although I feel like throwing up, I read. It's a big success. So much so that by the next day, I'm feeling the itch to start a new story. My chief disappointment with Bread Loaf is all the *talking* about writing and the lack of opportunity to actually *do* any.

Eventually I steal off to an Adirondack chair and jot a few sentences about a woman who is so poor that she's reduced to eating hangnail soup. What in the world does it *mean?* I think it mostly means that I've been biting my fingernails a lot up at Bread Loaf. Where will such weird writing lead me? I read what I've written over and over, and then, with confidence, I scratch each sentence out.

There aren't any extra points in life for being a writer. If a student finds that he wants to do something else, he should do it without feeling guilty. I mean, people talk about other people giving up writing as if they were failures. I don't think fishermen talk about other fishermen as failures who stop fishing and go into business instead. It's a strange thing. Many artists, writers, intellectuals, and academics really think that people who don't pursue these fields that test talent or test the mind are failures somehow or that something went wrong in their lives.

Thirty years after my first visit to Bread Loaf, I still carry in my wallet this simple souvenir: notations scribbled while I listened to a lecture given by the poet Marvin Bell.

I remember a genuine lightening within me as I copied Bell's words and fashioned a kind of quitter's permission slip, promising myself I could tender it anytime I wanted, and with grace, telling myself that quitting writing was a validation of sorts, too. A validation of the seeker's choice, not anybody else's.

Every now and then, I take the quote out to reread, then I tuck it respectfully away and keep going. It's my ticket to ride toward the respite of elsewhere, wherever that may be, but I've never felt the faintest wanderlust.

Seven

Creative Writing Class Noir

By the fall of 1976, my third semester at UNC–Chapel Hill, I've finally gained enough confidence to help my creative writing students revise a pretzeled sentence, but I'm not very good at discouraging the plodders and tin ears who write them. Who am I to lop somebody off from their aspirations? Plenty of people tried to lop me off from mine, but it didn't work. Max Steele, my boss, is a master lopper. "You do the untalented a big favor, lopping them off early enough so that they can go to medical or law school and make a decent living," he says. "I have an antique guillotine with a rusty blade in my office if you'd like to borrow it."

But it's hopeless. I'm comfortable untangling convoluted sentences or liberating tortured metaphors, but redirecting the students who write them makes me uneasy. I tell Max. "They're all so *young!* Who has the right to call them hopeless cases? They might get *better!*"

"Are they sick or just bad writers?" he asks. "Do they

need care or criticism? Maybe you're the one who ought to go to med school if you want to look after patients."

"I'm just a kinder person than you," I say, and he laughs, so genuinely happy to be the meanest among us that I laugh too.

"The only benefit of being kind to your students instead of ruthless is that you won't risk making some lunatic mad," he says. "There are lots of lunatics in creative writing classes. You'll see. Or maybe you won't. Maybe your kindness will keep them at bay. But I doubt it. I think it will probably attract them like flies to honey."

I do want to move tenderly among the students like some Florence Nightingale, although I know my own best teachers had brusque bedside manners: Miss Joyner in high school, calling out to our English class as she passed back papers, "Will somebody loan Marianne a pencil? Poor thing's run out of decent ink and keeps filling her fountain pen with Welch's grape juice. It's making her prose purple!" Or Fred Chappell in graduate school, speechless with dismay, giving my manuscript such a gloomy look that the pages in his hands seemed to wither and blacken, as good-for-nothing as banana peels.

I'd like to be as comfortable giving the thumbs-down signal as the thumbs-up, and with colossal inconsistency, I try. But it's just not me. Most days I don't know what I'm doing, except going through the motions of some Great Pretender, the mockingbird of creative writing teachers.

I once peered into a mockingbird's nest and found it valiantly inventive: twinkling chewing-gum wrappers, a peppermint-striped soda straw, a pipe cleaner, and one spent balloon dangling from a string, all woven like decorations through the basics of twigs and straw. Like statements of personal taste, artistic flair, a bohemian personality. It was a nest all right, but somehow you didn't quite trust that what had built it was a bird. So how can my students trust my opinion on any given day when it feels so experimental and makeshift, my performance so patchy and *borrowed*? I like the *idea* of teaching college, of course, because it feels like having stature, whether I deserve that or not. I like the challenge to my intellect and my natural timidity and being around bright people who listen respectfully and do not throw spitballs. But any student who does not throw spitballs has already endeared himself to me.

I am twenty-eight years old, and part of my Great Pretender syndrome derives from the fact that I look the same age as my students. I slouch at my desk, same as them, wearing my jeans, hippie headscarves, and John Lennon-esque wire-rimmed glasses. I bum their cigarettes. In 1976 nearly everybody smokes; there are built-in ashtrays in all the classroom desks, and nobody apologizes if they can't make it through an hour-long class without caving in to a nicotine fit. Smoking is *cool*—sort of the last dangerous thing you can do in public and not get arrested. It feels congenial, sitting around puffing away with the students, discussing Kafka's "The Hunger Artist" and appearing more confident and authoritative than you really are, gesturing with your cigarette baton. Then Johnny Mateer comes swashbuckling into class.

Johnny's about my age but he looks much older, even without the prop of a cigarette. He's handsome in a knavish way, with wavy, chocolate-colored hair and a thick mustache. His skin looks ruddy with windburn. Even sitting at his desk he appears to be leaning into a stiff sea breeze, squinting at the horizon with the penetrating glance of somebody who sees better and farther *without* binoculars. He wears blousy white peasant shirts open at the throat, black jeans, and pirate boots. The word *bucca-*

JOHNNY MATEER

neer comes to mind. Count of Monte Cristo. Prisoner of Chillon. You can tell he knows about shadowy things that the rest of the class does not by the way he sits apart from us, keeping his serious captain's vigil, careful not to get sucked into the undertow of our triviality.

Up until now, I've been pretending to be a teacher in front of college kids. But Johnny Mateer is a *man.* One afternoon I wind up standing behind him in the checkout line at Kerr Drugs. He looks particularly vivid under the fluorescent lights, out of place, like wildlife. "Oh, hi, Johnny," I say in a meekling's voice. It's the way I would talk to a bear or a wolf. Standing there, sort of *looming,* actually, waiting for the line to inch along, he's no better at small talk than I am. I'm struggling not to cast my snoopy, writer's fodder-gathering eyes in the direction of his purchases, but there's this weird, spotlighted sensation of beckoning in my peripheral vision. It's like when you're a kid and there's a total eclipse of the sun and you've been told that under no circumstances is it safe to stare at the eclipse or the radioactive glare will cook your retinas and shrivel your eyes like raisins, but it feels almost like the blindness might be worth a glimpse of something so rare and forbidden. So I look. Worse, he sees me look. I'm *blind!* My *eyes!* The cashier appears to be ringing up about ten thousand condoms.

It's the era of Farrah Fawcett-Majors posters, Bob Marley's reggae. You can pick out the sorority girls on campus by their shiny, wholesome Dorothy Hamill haircuts. Movie marquees on Franklin Street in downtown Chapel Hill herald *Rocky* and *Network* and Stephen King's *Carrie.* I don't see *Carrie.* Horror is beneath me. Stephen King is beneath me. If it's not in *The Norton Anthology of Literature,* I don't have time to read it.

On television there's *Bionic Woman, Charlie's Angels,* and *Wonder Woman,* exalting women who assert themselves—physically, not intellectually. There's *The Gong Show,* teaching everybody how *not* to indulge the untalented. It's also a strangely confessional, embarrassingly honest time. Post-Watergate, people have started telling *too* much. Jimmy Carter gets elected president and, having promised never to tell a lie, gives his infamous *Playboy* interview in which he admits to looking on a number of random women with lust. "I've committed adultery in my heart many times," he says.

Tom Wolfe, writing in *New York* magazine, dubs the 1970s the "Me Decade." No surprise that the stories my students write are largely self-referential: rueful tales of dorm life, blind dates, frat-party shenanigans. There are homegrown stories too: lots of oracular grandmothers sitting in rocking chairs and snapping green beans. It's what they all *know*, and I've encouraged them to write from experience, not churn out the gothic, melodramatic glop I did when I was their age: stories that employed every shock effect I could devise to distract the reader from the miserable writing itself. Then, one day, Johnny Mateer, who is usually quiet in class, still pretty much a stranger in our midst, turns in a different sort of story that blows the lid off the familiar and mundane.

The story takes place in a Moroccan prison and describes the despicable conditions: dirt floors, no sanitation or privacy, overcrowding, stifling heat, sleeplessness, food a cockroach could barely survive on. How does Johnny know about such things? It's a couple of decades before you can trawl the Internet for exotic information. In a California garage, two amateur electronics geeks are still at work inventing the Apple computer. "Because those things really happened to me," he says.

Fall break comes and goes and we reassemble—without Johnny Mateer. He never returns, and there's no word on why. A revision of the Moroccan prison story is not forthcoming, so, at term's end, I record his grade as an "Incomplete." If he contacts me and makes up his missed work within a certain time frame, his "IN" will convert to an A, because clearly an A for Authentic is what he deserves.

There are any number of reasons he might have stopped coming to class (it occurs to me that his massive expenditure for condoms may have taken precedence over paying the tuition bill). But of course the thought does flicker across my mind on the dreadful dark wings of doubt that he stopped coming to class because he believed there was nothing I could teach him.

By spring term 1977, I've been teaching long enough to have earned a reputation for kindness. Lunatic bait, Max calls me. Between classes, my office fills with students seeking commiseration about life in general as well as help with their writing. No wonder it's hard for me to get any of my own creative work done. The students are simply more fascinating than any words I might pile on the page. Who needs to *create* drama when you've got all these eager, living stories in the shapes of human beings walking around? Many are treading dangerous waters, barely keeping their heads above the black lagoons of depression, drugs, alcohol addiction, abusive relationships, family turmoil, promiscuity, impoverishment, debt, anxiety disorders (I hear you, brothers and sisters!), and, yes—lunacy. It's hard not to detect lunacy's ripple effect throughout the entire culture, what with the recently captured "Son of Sam" confessing that he murdered people on orders from a talking dog and devoted fans claiming to see Elvis (who has died, but not really, not *ever*) everywhere.

One morning, less than a week into the semester, a tall raggedy scarecrow of a boy barrels into class late, heaves himself into a chair, and announces he's newly enrolled. The other students have been telling anecdotes about their holiday vacations, so I invite the newcomer to tell one too. "You don't want to hear my story," he says, then leaps to his feet and launches into a tirade against his girlfriend, who dumped him over the weekend for a lesbian lover. Now he's yelling, red-faced, apoplectic, hurling anatomical descriptions, spewing fiendish scatological detail, spit flying from his mouth, drops of perspiration as big as

THE MAD EVANGELIST

thumbtacks studding his forehead. He's pacing, squinting through tears, flailing his arms, and cursing like a mad evangelist of porn. *Do something,* the other students, a pale blur of hostage faces, telepath to me. I can't budge. I'm as terrified as if held at gunpoint. But the bell *does* ring. Mercifully there used to be bells along with ashtrays.

As the students flee, the jilted boy simmers down. He's mumbling to himself now, still pacing, wiping his eyes with the backs of his hands. I step forward—I don't know what for, because I'm too unnerved to know the right gesture to make. One touch and he might bite me. But when I look into his eyes, it's like looking into a swamp. He doesn't know I'm there, doesn't see me. He gathers and bundles the sharp splinters of himself, bolts out the door, and is gone.

"Go tell Professor Gaskin," Max says when I inform him about the incident.

Professor Gaskin, appointed to succeed zany Bill Harmon as chairperson of the English department, is himself about as zany as a pheasant under glass. He's an elegant, soft-spoken older gentleman who seems to have walked out of one of Edith Wharton's drawing rooms.

"Tell him everything you just told me," Max says.

"No way. You mean the filthy language?"

"Every word of it."

"I can't do it. I can't say those terrible words to Professor Gaskin."

"You said them to me."

"*You* tell him. Professor Gaskin is like some sweet old turtle grandfather."

Max is looking at me like *I'm* the lunatic.

"I'll go with you," he says. "But you're going to tell him. They're just words."

"Maybe I overreacted. Maybe it wasn't that bad," I say. "He was probably high, and now that the drug's worn off, he's mortified. Or maybe it wasn't drugs. Maybe he was justifiably upset. He needed a place to blow off steam, and now that he's done he'll be a model citizen."

"I wouldn't bet on it," Max says, picking up the phone to call Gaskin. On the way downstairs to his office, I practice saying the heinous words until they sound as harmless as *Betty Botter bought some butter.* Well, not quite. Judging from the hardening-into-granite look of Professor Gaskin's face when I repeat the words to him, they have not lost their shock value.

Next time the class meets, both Gaskin and Max are

waiting outside the door like hit men disguised as college administrators. They're wearing coats and ties and concrete faces. The tall, wild, muddy-eyed boy comes stomping down the hall in his Jack the Teacher-Killer boots, and they step out of the shadows and collar him. He's so quickly dispatched, it's as if one of them were brandishing a shepherd's crook. There's not one yelp or snarl of protest. All three of them simply whoosh into the netherworld of campus disciplinary procedures, and the boy does not return. Whatever punishment the authorities devise chews up and swallows the guy. He's banned from entering our kingdom *forever.* How do they manage this? It's like *Out, out, damn spot,* and the spot's gone. Doesn't hurt their cause that in 1977 the Supreme Court rules that teachers spanking schoolchildren for misbehavior is constitutional.

A couple of years later I recognize the ousted one panhandling on Franklin Street. He's grown a bushy Moses beard and is sitting cross-legged on a blanket that he's spread on the sidewalk in front of a bank. He's strumming a guitar and wearing those shabby fingerless half-gloves that remind me of the sad-sack poverty of a Dickens orphan. He's flipped open a banged-up instrument case to receive spare change. Whether true or not, the circumstances in which I find him lead me to conclude that getting kicked out of my class was the beginning of his downfall. I don't feel like the Professor of Kind anymore.

Here's my biggest question about the people who tend to go haywire in creative writing classes: Are they crazy to begin with, or is it something we stand for or do in class that allows their lunacy a platform, that sets them off? I begin to wonder if some comment about his Moroccan prison story pushed Johnny Mateer over the edge, some excruciating divide he sensed between his larger life of experience and our small, snug innocence that gave him pause. Maybe he'd begun to feel squirrelly, to sense the claustrophobia of domestication when he was born to live wild. Who were we to sit in judgment of his adventure story, no matter how positive that judgment turned out to be? Writing workshops are filled with kindly nitpickers, but nitpickers all the same.

I once caught a squirrel in a Hav-a-Hart trap. The squirrel had been trapped in my attic for days and wouldn't be lured by peanut butter. It occurred to me that he might be thirsting to death, so I baited the trap with a bowl of water, and it worked. He went for it, and I captured him humanely. But by the time I'd carried the cage outside to release the animal, he'd clobbered his head so maniacally against the bars, trying to break free, that he'd scalped himself, and he staggered away across the grass dazed and bleeding, more victimized by my trying to do the right thing than freed.

By the time I've met a few others, I suspect that Johnny Mateer was my first lunatic but that I was too naïve those early semesters and didn't recognize the symptoms: a certain detachment from the group, a glimmer of preoccupation in his eyes, scanning an imaginary vista, yearning to see more than it's possible to see. Then, there was his mysterious disappearance. Had I romanticized a person who should have made me wary? Was it possible that he'd cribbed his Moroccan prison tale from a story by Camus or Paul Bowles? Had the ten thousand condoms I'd watched him buy been intended for some enterprise so profoundly illegal that I didn't have the worldliness to imagine it?

Every semester those first few years after Johnny Mateer vanishes, I attract a lunatic or two. Some of them wrap their little bat wings around themselves and cope; others explode. Max boasts that he rarely attracts them anymore. The few who wander into his class he spots early and scares away before they can latch on. Such detection requires vigilant paranoia, but Max says paranoia is as dependable a survival tactic as any. My other seasoned colleagues, Daphne Athas and Doris Betts, don't attract many lunatics either, or they're simply better at folding them into the mix than I. Daphne's far too busy being cosmic to distinguish them from the normal students, and Doris is the Obi-Wan Kenobi of our program. She can halt a hissing volcano with one wink of her gimlet eye and speak such spellbinding words that the troublemaker, forgetting he ever wanted to take a creative writing class in the first place, trundles off to become a missionary instead.

My theory is that the creative writing program attracts lunatics because those of us in it are not rank-and-file academicians. Only Max and Doris have tenure. The rest of us lecturers, hired semester by semester, share a kind of outsiders' antiestablishment belief that lesser gods—which we are by dint of departmental hierarchy and our unanimous lack of doctoral degrees—don't have much to lose. Academia encourages eccentricity, but we who occupy the bottom rung feel a kind of permission to flaunt ours. Perhaps the crazies recognize us as sympathizers because, like them, we're fringe. Our classes are intimate and cozy, more like burrows than the chilly echo chambers of lecture halls. We learn each other's names. We discuss and advise rather than pontificate. We laugh a lot and indulge as much as we lambaste. We sit around the seminar table like a group of friends at dinner, dishing out stories, not food, but the scene is still ragtag communal.

Spring semester 1978, I don't spot Chuck Tabor as a troublemaker except in some smart-alecky frat-boy way. He's burly, moon-faced, bored-looking, walks with a

Chuck Tabor

MY PERFECT STORY

splay-footed swagger like somebody stuffed from an all-you-can-eat buffet. His writing swaggers and yammers too, and he's about as interested in improving it as he is in polishing his shoes. Polishing anything is servant stuff; that's the aura he gives off. He wears khaki shorts and deck shoes without socks, even in frigid weather. *Yeah, Weather, it's Chuck Tabor here, so fuck you!*

So, one day we're workshopping his first story. He's tilted back in his chair with a cocksure pose of dueness, as if he's expecting maid service along with our critiques. So I get out the abrasive cleaner, so to speak, and start scouring. First I point out all the technical mistakes in the manuscript: the run-on sentences, misspellings, sloppy margins, thumbprints, typos, changes in point of view.

"OK, OK, OK," Chuck says. "It's a draft, OK? All that stuff can be fixed."

He's written about a game of golf. I ask if he intended to write a whole story or just a descriptive scene.

"Oh, it's a story all right," he says. "It's a story about playing golf."

"Who are the players? Does one of them want to win the game more than the other one? Is there a conflict?"

"It's two Delta Sigs, OK? They *both* want to win. Like, *duh.*" He looks around the room, smirking, like, *isn't this teacher the biggest dumbass y'all ever saw?*

"Who or what changes?"

Chuck guffaws. He can't believe how stupid I am. "The *conflict* is will the ball go in the hole, and *what changes* is the wind. *No*, the ball will not go in the hole. The *wind* puffs it away."

He's so defensive that everyone's clammed up except me. Long silences make me squirm. "Are the men disappointed?" I know that I am asking stupid questions because it's a stupid nonstory and because it's not written by a storyteller anyway but by somebody bored out of his skull by the assignment and doing homework half-assed.

"*No*, the *men* are *not* disappointed. They'd just as soon *go drink a beer.*" Chuck's fidgeting with a pencil, glancing around the room now, trying to make eye contact with any classmate who agrees. "Come *on, y'all,*" he yells. "It's just a *damn story* about a *damn golf game*! Leave it *alone!*"

His face is as red as a cherry bomb. Before anybody can respond, he shoves back his chair, springs from the seat, grabs and lifts the chair and slams it against the seminar table. He spears an accusing finger at me. "*Who the HELL are you* to tell me WHAT THE SHIT is wrong with MY story?

Huh? *WHO THE HELL PUT YOU IN CHARGE? WHAT'S
SO GREAT ABOUT YOU?"* With every word, he lurches
toward me, just barely in control so that the lurching does
not transport him into a full-powered launch. But I can tell
that he's warming up for a launch, making ready to hurdle
the table between us any second and wring my scrawny
professorial neck.

I'm not aware there are other people still in the room
until Lynette Iezzoni, Superhero—a girl who looks like
Botticelli painted her onto the world, the best writer and
most thoughtful critic in the class, a writer who will go
on to author a highly praised book about the Spanish
influenza—materializes, steps inside Chuck's burning ring
of fire, and lays her tender hand upon his arm. "Shush,"
she says softly. "It's OK. Nobody meant to upset you."

The instant she speaks, Chuck's transformed from beast
into tortured frat boy again. He snatches his story from the
table and tears out of the room. When he gets back to his
room, he torches the manuscript and sets the room on fire.

I never hear from him or see him again. But his battle
cry—part accusation, part impotent outrage, part damn
good questions—has resonated throughout my career as
teacher, critic, and writer. Its echo still has the power to
stop me in my rush-to-judgment tracks.

Late in the spring of 1978, I receive a copy of a letter
addressed to the Dean of Arts and Sciences. Written
March 30, 1977, it has been in transit for more than a year.
Scribbled in legible, if imperfect, French, the letter, having
gotten past the censors at Prison Civile in Casablanca, is
from Johnny Mateer.

*Je vous ecris concernant plusieurs de cours (incompletes) que je ne
finissais pas l'automme de 1976 . . . j'vais la chance revinir a Marac
[Morocco] acheter de la merchandise pour Andrean Imports . . .*

He is writing about his "Incompletes" in courses taken at UNC in the fall of 1976, when he also seized the opportunity to return to Morocco to buy merchandise for an import company. He pleads for an extension so that he can "make up" work needed to finish the courses. He's in jail again. No telling how long he's been there or when he will be liberated. *J'espere que serai libere plutot,* he writes ("I hope to be freed soon"). But that was more than a year ago and the letter has just now arrived. What if he's still in some slimy, rat-infested Moroccan cell? My writer's brain goes into feeding-frenzy mode.

What if writing that letter was the equivalent of the one phone call a person jailed in the United States gets to make? What if it was an attempt to alert a savvy recipient about the urgency of the situation? Was the letter a coded plea for diplomatic intervention?

J'vais tres envie revinir ici m'aides ecrive un roman de les experiences que j'avais ici il y a quatres ans (J'habitais ici pour deux ans). En partirant de Casablanca, les douanes me cherchuient comme d'habitude et trouvient mes notes, et aussi une histoire que j'avais ecriver pour Marianne Gingher (Eng. 23W, ecrive creatif) qui avait les implications politique . . .ils me jettient en prison pour les reasons politiques . . . .

Roughly translated, he writes that he was eager to return to Morocco in order to facilitate writing a novel about his experiences there—he'd previously lived there for two years. When he was leaving Casablanca, customs officers searched his belongings and found the notes for his novel and the story he had written in my class. The authorities had judged the story to be politically subversive and arrested him. *Mon Dieu!*

I phone the dean's office, but nobody there has read the Moroccan prison story and knows Johnny's political vulnerabilities the way I believe I do. I recall hearing dark tales about American hippies traveling in that part of the world being sentenced to life imprisonment or, worse, *executed* for possessing a single leaf of marijuana.

The mystery of what happened to Johnny Mateer in the intervening months since our acquaintance has finally been solved for me but in an unsettling, incomplete way. What more do I do about it? Well, here's perhaps the biggest mystery of all: I tuck the letter away. I postpone further investigation and do nothing. I don't have the time; I don't have the resources. I rationalize that the dean has informed all relevant or significant parties of Johnny's whereabouts. I'm caught up in the problems of my current crop of creative writer types. And they're all weird or unique or incarcerated (psychologically speaking) in some way. Too, I'm up to my eyebrows in personal stuff. My husband is finishing up his Ph.D. and looking for a teaching job, but there aren't any. Meanwhile, in fits and starts, I'm *forcing* myself to try writing a novel, whether I've got an idea for one or not. It seems like everybody is writing a novel. Even the typewriter mechanic, a Vietnam vet who services my husband's IBM Selectric, is writing one.

Over the next twenty-five years or so, I get lots of mileage out of the Moroccan prison story, but whenever I include it in a lecture, inevitably somebody in the audience will ask, "Did you ever find out if he got out of jail?"

"No, I never did," I confess, and wince a little because it seems I am cheating, using the story to supplement some point I'm trying to make about the dangers and risks of writing the truth when I've only discovered part of it. For years I delight in surprising my listeners with the delicious irony of something as benign as a college writing assignment leading to such a harrowing experience for its author. And once, when I'm asked to speak at an American

Civil Liberties Union gathering, I talk about Johnny Mateer's incarceration as an example of what happens in a country where basic freedoms of speech and press are not protected. But *what do I really know? Who the hell put me in charge of anybody else's story?* I hear their chorus of indictment, all those student lunatics I have known, forever demanding that I be accountable, as if claiming sanity obligates me to be. And from my audience, again, the question: "Did he ever get out of jail?"

Not long ago, with the help of one superlative administrative assistant and the Internet, I sleuth out several Johnny Mateers some living on the West Coast and others in Florida, all near the sea. Although none of their particulars seem a likely match, I'm eager to try making contact. And then my assistant discovers Johnny's elderly parents are still living—and where.

I phone Mr. Mateer on a Sunday afternoon. "Well, now, isn't that the nicest thing?" he responds eagerly. "Imagine after all these years, a teacher who would care enough to call." We talk for nearly an hour.

When we finally hang up, I know the following: that Johnny was always different from his sisters; that he was always the restless one, smart as the others but never quite able to niche himself in any long-term respectable way. Dropped out of college and never went back. Took various itinerant jobs and got fired because he had problems taking orders. Got into trouble with the law. Traveled around Europe. Got into trouble selling drugs. Married an Italian woman. Went to prison in Morocco—twice. The second time he was in jail for seven months. Was brought back to the States by U.S. marshals. Did some jail time in California. Got interested in religious cults and joined one for a while. After divorcing the Italian, he married another girl and ran a construction business in the Pacific Northwest. Business went bust. Ended up in the Philippines, where he planned to mine gold. Didn't find any. Now lives with a Filipino woman he met there, and they have two sons. "I've never met her," Mr. Mateer tells me. "I never met his other wives either, except the Italian. She was nice, but she didn't know what she was in for, marrying Johnny."

"But he survived the Moroccan prison ordeal," I say. It seems the least of his trials.

"Oh, yes. Now, he's a survivor. You can say that for him."

"He was a good writer," I say.

"Is that so? Isn't that nice of you to say?"

"I always wanted to know what happened to him."

"Well, now, isn't that something that you'd take the trouble to call? I appreciate that, I really do."

"Next time you talk with him, please tell him I called."

There's a pause, then Mr. Mateer says, "I don't talk to him much anymore. His mother calls him every now and then, but you see, Johnny is always asking for money. If you call him, he'll ask you to send a little along. And we always do, of course, but we don't call too much because of that."

"I understand."

"It's not that I don't love my son and think of him. I do love Johnny, but he's been our difficult child. You love them anyway, don't you? And we'd do anything for any of them if we could. But Johnny is somebody you don't get in touch without him asking for something."

I thank Mr. Mateer for his time and he thanks me for mine. "Really nice talking to you about Johnny," he says. "That makes my day, to think that after all these years you'd still remember a student like him. I love him, don't get me wrong, but he's still a mystery to me. I guess some mysteries you just have to learn to live with."

Eight

The Southern Writer Thing

I don't know what else to call it. Niche? Genre? Cult? The word *Thing* is as slippery as the word *Southern*— which I guess is my point. I don't even think of myself as a Southern Writer until somebody calls me one. Is it a good thing? A bad thing? A straitjacket thing? Does it bring Faulkner and Welty instantly to mind—or *The Dukes of Hazard* and Moon Pies? Can you choose *not* to be a Southern writer if you grow up in the South?

Summer of 1978, I hie myself up to New York City to meet Ginger Barber, a literary agent interested in representing my short stories. Her agency is located on Greenwich Avenue, more than fifty blocks from the friend's apartment on Central Park South where I'm staying. I don't know anything about finding my way around New York, but somebody tells me that if I just keep walking down the Avenue of the Americas, I'll eventually get wherever I'm going.

There's nothing like walking in New York to make a

rube delusional, convince her that she's belonged there her whole life. You get the feeling that nobody's a stranger for long in a place that seethes with strangeness. It's alive! It's alive! Everything's huffing and puffing, tooting, whooshing, bashing, screeching, rattling, gleaming: the horns, the wind, the windowpanes, flags, my hair, sirens, pigeons, police galloping on horseback, subway maws, somebody's hat, somebody's temper. At every cross street I twirl myself around the lamppost. Bright blue shards of windchime sky shimmer and ching between the looming buildings. In the streets snappish taxis lurch and tangle like schools of yellow sharks. A boom box squalls past so loud that I may have swallowed it. In the roar and heft of this splendid tumult, I'm as skippy as a Dixie cup.

When I arrive at 44 Greenwich Avenue, Mary Evans, Ginger's assistant, buzzes me up. It's a long flight of stairs to their plain little office, but there they are, leaning inquisitive faces over the banister, smiling, waiting to greet me with such warmth and hospitality I could be a long-lost relative. "You walked?" they cry. "It's too hot to walk! Gosh, doesn't she *look* Southern?" one of them says.

Do they mean that it was a dumb thing to walk? Why do I think that?

On the way to eat lunch in the Village, I catch sight of my reflection in a storefront window. *Do* I look Southern? What does a Southerner look like? Minnie Pearl? Aunt Jemima? Daisy Duke? A bumpkin? It's not as if I'm wearing the Confederate flag. I have on a sleeveless madras dress, my sturdy red leather sandals, a navy blue ribbon tied around my neck like a choker, my yellow straw Breton and sunglasses—big round ones like Audrey Hepburn wore in *Breakfast at Tiffany's.* Maybe it's the hat. The hat's on a string. I lift it off my forehead, flip it backwards, and wear it bobbing against my shoulder blades for the

DO I LOOK SOUTHERN?

duration of our meeting. I suddenly wish I hadn't worn it. Nobody else in Greenwich Village is wearing a yellow straw Breton. Now that I notice, when the wind hits the brim at a certain slant, the hat *twangs.* Oh, dear.

Ginger's a stouthearted Southerner herself (or so she pretends) from tiny Galax, Virginia, but she's lived in the Northeast so long that she can pass for one of Them. She talks about the South as if it's hallowed ground. I worry that maybe she's trying to trick me, acting all crackerish herself, hoping I'll loosen up and reveal my white trash soul. The Age of Political Correctness is dawning, and I have a hunch that being Southern verges on the wobblymost edge of correct. Ginger's too sophisticated to want a Yahoo for a client, but I fake her out with my dessert selection. She's betting I'll get the watermelon or some clodhopper banana pudding. But I go for the bilberries and cream. I pronounce it, trilling the r's. What *are* bilberries anyway? I'm pretty sure Uncle Remus doesn't grow them. Meanwhile, I'm crisping up my language when I talk so I won't sound like a mush-mouth. I enunciate each word with tidy precision, my tongue as snugly checked as a sheet made up with hospital corners. I am so stressed-out trying not to look or act or speak too Southern that somehow, during dessert, I twitch my sandals off my feet and lose them under the table. Where are they? I'm trying to manage a discreet minesweep with my outstretched legs, and when it's time to leave the restaurant, I'm still groping. The sandals have splayed themselves so far apart that it seems they're running away. When I finally snag them and slip them back on and walk out of the restaurant alongside Ginger, I realize something worse has happened. I've gotten them on the wrong feet! Do I stop to switch them and admit my bumpkinhood plain as day? I'm clomping valiantly along like a drunk in a pair of rubber flippers, but I bid Ginger as dignified a farewell as I can muster. To do otherwise would concede too much ground to the bumbling stereotype of Southernness I've tried vigorously to avoid. Damn that turkey-in-the-straw Breton hat, thumping against my shoulders as I slouch my prideful, slew-footed self home towards Central Park!

I'm invited to give a reading at the University of Vermont. Thanks to my sponsors, the assembly room is packed—a miraculous turnout for an unknown writer. I would be wrecked with stage fright if not for the warmth of this eager, attentive crowd. The faces beaming up at me look uniformly balmy. I feel as welcomed as a hometown girl. But I am not a hometown girl, as my introducer makes clear. I am a *Southern* writer, and the instant I hear the words, I feel cast off on to some nether shelf of literature, albeit gently, and niched in a pile of old tried-and-true stuff gathered up for Goodwill.

I've picked a humorous story to read—always a gamble but even more so this far from the Mason-Dixon. Corral a bunch of New Englanders to hear a Southerner read comedy and something's bound to get lost in translation. What if they think that a hush puppy is some kind of meat?

So I'm reading merrily along, and, sure, I think the story is funny, but I'm a Southern writer, remember, and the stuff Down Here isn't always funny Up There. These folks are whacking their thighs with delight. They're body-slamming each other with glee, laughing so hard they're spewing tears. Gosh, they start howling even before I get to a paragraph's punch lines. Did I just hear a Rebel yell? I have never in my life had a rowdier response from an audience of strangers.

It's not until the reception, when some innocent admirer comments on my hilarious delivery, that I apprehend the audience hadn't been laughing at the story. They were laughing at the way I *read* the story, my accent, my drawl, at the cornpone crawly swamp cat Tar baby hee-haw julipy sugahpie sound of my *voice.* I have never felt more like a Southern writer for all the wrong reasons.

All of which gets me going on a lifetime of excuses and defenses regarding why I am *not* a Southern writer. Or not *entirely* one. Or, if I am, then I'm a hapless, quirky version, not standard issue. Well, who likes to flaunt a big *S* on their chest all the time, except Superman?

Because if it *is* some sort of membership by conscription in a club, this Southern Writer *Thang,* can we ever be *separate* and equal? Both from one another and from all the rest? I've never met a writer who likes being lumped and blended.

Once, when asked what distinguished her as a Southern writer, the novelist and essayist Blanche McCrary Boyd wisecracked, "Crunchy vegetables."

Huh?

"I don't like them and I don't eat them," she said.

It's true that writers not raised on Southern soul food prefer crisp, salutable, ramrod beans. Whereas Blanche and I hanker after beans slow-cooked all day: squishy, gummable, and redolent with ham hock.

I don't know why we cook our beans all day Down Here. Unless we have all day to do it. Maybe they don't have all day Up There. Of course, I'm only guessing, but I want to get to the bottom of this Southern Thing, too, and maybe our unique food choices are the key. Who knows how the culinary preferences of writers starve or nourish their muses? You are what you eat, somebody once said. Maybe I wouldn't talk and act and write the way I do if I had never stood over a pot of beans for five or six hours, patiently stirring and coddling.

The humorist Roy Blount Jr. owns that now and again we Southerners do crave a taste of good dirt. It tastes a shade better than crow, but crow's pretty good, too. Did he say that or did I? After a while, if you're Southern, who said what tends to get all mixed up in the great clacking Crock-Pot of our collective craw.

But if it's not the food, what is it that unites us? Our penchant for the superfluous word? The adventures of digression? Behold the geranium flush called forth by the high-octane intoxicants of verbosity: rumor, anecdote, gossip, fable, argument, and outright lie.

It's been suggested that Southerners are *natural* talkers

DIRT
(YUM!)

and that our talk grows out of a kind of delirium produced by our exposure to protracted summer heat. Because what else is there to do on a sluggish, late September Dog Day (when Northerners are enjoying their first bracing frosts of the season and Westerners, their early light snow) but languish on the front-porch glider, rubbing our sweaty faces in a late-grown watermelon, spitting seeds, listening out? If we're listening out, we're bound to hear something—even if it's just the neighbor's kids playing in the water sprinkler. And if what we hear isn't particularly newsworthy, let's fix it so it is. Have one of the kids almost drown. Nobody expects the truth from us in such a punishment of weather. The heat pretty much turns everyone into invalids, cranky and bored. So talk: *a kid almost drowns in the water sprinkler.* Sure, it's a stretch of the imagination, but nothing else feels like stretching, so why not? Remember to talk slowly. Eke it out. We don't want our lips to work up a sweat.

Slowness is part of the Southern Thing. You can't take seriously the folks who demean it. Slowness is the pace of wonder. Even our lightning bugs are slow, drawling their light as they amble across a Southern dusk. Up north, the lightning bugs I've observed put on a glitzy show, flashing like strobes. I've pointed this out to my New England friends, but they think I'm exaggerating the difference, boasting of absurd *Faulknerian* stream-of-consciousness lightning bugs, while theirs jump around like party dudes. But it's true. Southern lightning bugs waltz heavily across the twilight, as if drunk, slurring their light, little lost miners of darkness carrying lanterns with faulty wicks. Their hasty Northern counterparts seem to have beaten them to the diamonds and go flinging their treasure into the night with spendthrift abandon.

How we do carry on about the littlest of things.

The urge to delve, the urge to captivate an audience, exists in every storyteller. But, for Southerners, it's often moderated by a conscientious effort to remember who you aim to inform or accommodate. After all, without an audience, you're left drawling in the dark.

We Southerners may be slow. We may be trivial and just as villainous as the law allows. We may eat dirt and cook our food to mush and lie more twisted than a braided rug. But we are an infinitely patient species, and we know how to indulge each other.

Which is why, in the South, we will encourage, say, the long-winded tale we get at some crossroads filling station, when all we've asked this man in a town of three stoplights is how to find, and find quickly, the local university campus where a poetry reading by a gifted native son is already in progress. But this grease-splotched man, this man who wouldn't think of inconveniencing you with self-serve pumps, has a *story* he's yearning to tell. He's lived in this town all his life. Knows the place so well and inside out that he can't tell you how to navigate five blocks of it without expansive, whirlwind gestures. In a small place, the logistics of movement are more complex than you've ever dreamed. You need a sense of this town's *whole history* to get around it. "You want to drive to the whole other side of town," the man says grandly, arcing his arm. "You're *way* aways."

It's perspective, see. Southernness is all about the *potential*, the largesse and bounty—not the thrift—of small-ness. "Look," the man says, "you're bound to get mixed up at the intersection of General and Lee streets. It's a jumble ever since they made Ulysses Road one way. Why they gone and done that? They done the same with Peace and Sweet Gum, the streets you take to the cemetery, if you got some reason to go there, and it's none of my business if you do or you don't. So if you want to get to—won't it the university you asked about?—it's kindly uphill, and a ziggityzag to boot. Nobody's got used to it, even us what lives here. Now the graveyard's between Sweet Gum and Peace. Probably they made the one-ways out of respect. Less traffic. Less noise to bother the mourners going in and out with their mourning to do. But now you head past the cemetery on Sweet Gum, and where it forks at Proximity and Divine, you take you the middle fork on that no-name road. I know what you're thinking. Whoever heard of a middle fork? Well, lady, we got us a middle fork here."

So I'm starting to feel more comfortable about the Southern Thing, even a tad illuminated. Maybe it's less of a Thing than a trumpet vine. Or a tree. A big old gnarly family tree: magnolia-esque and bosomy with blooms. Sometimes you're glad for its shelter. Other times when you flit from its branches, you're thankful it's checked by roots and can't chase and consume you. Or can it? Those roots disappearing into the depths of the planet are as thick and scary as alligator tails, but will they hold?

One summer, I travel back to Vermont to teach at Bennington College. Upon arrival, I discover that the airline has lost my luggage. I fill out some forms at the airport and take a cab to the college. I'm missing my casual clothes, toothbrush, books, notebooks, my lucky fountain pen, my blow-dryer, my Oil of Olay. My skin goes *scritch* without Oil of Olay.

When I reach the campus cottage where I'm to lodge for two weeks, the first person I spot is a stranger— another Southern writer whose face I recognize from the conference catalog photo. It's Blanche McCrary Boyd, devotee of the cooked-to-mush green bean. She's driven her car from Connecticut, where she teaches, and is busily unpacking a trunkload of homey-looking items: a Mr. Coffee machine, a set of mugs, a portable fan, aluminum lawn chairs, beach towels, multiple six-packs of Diet Coke. I feel myself overcome by the sort of wistfulness I felt as a child, away at camp, for the amenities of home. I miss my suitcase desperately—but not unutterably. No, *never* that!

"Hello!" I call to this woman who is clad in a T-shirt, comfy shorts, and sensible running shoes. I feel stockaded in my travelogue outfit: a constricting sheath of a dress and torture-chamber high heels. "Lucky you drove!" I tell her. "You've brought all your nesting materials. Me, I had this loop-the-loop trip on U.S. Air. You wouldn't have believed the stewardess—a genuine wacko. When she got on the microphone to give us safety tips about the oxygen masks and so forth, she said, I kid you not, 'If you're traveling with a child or if you're traveling with someone who just *acts* like one. . . .' Anyway, the plane was delayed in Washington for three hours. Then, I get here and discover my luggage did not. I had the greatest pair of earrings in that suitcase. I'd ordered them from California—they're made out of bottle caps with little photos of George, Paul, John, and Ringo inside the caps. Anyway, those earrings along with this new story I've been working on, 'Plutonium

Pie,' are probably all gone with the wind. Damn! It was my only copy of that story, too. It's about a husband and wife having a total meltdown over making a pie together. Gee, I haven't even introduced myself to you yet. Where are my manners? Why am I telling you all this stuff?"

She gives me a sisterly look of bemused tolerance. "I guess because you're Southern," she says.

Nine

Thrill Life with Child

In the spring of 1978, after completing his Ph.D. in English, my husband decides he doesn't want to teach college English after all. He thinks he might want to be a CPA or go for a business degree and climb the corporate ladder. Possibly he can write *his* Great American Novel on the side.

He signs up to take an accounting class and discovers, once and for all, that he's no good with numbers—but then balancing a checkbook has never inspired him much either. Next, he investigates the feasibility of pursuing an undergraduate degree in biology, the prerequisite he'll need before he signs up for the M-CAT exams and (if he scores high enough) applies to medical school. He's thirty-three; he'll be forty-three or so before he finishes his M.D., an internship, residency, then sets up a practice. Do you know how old forty-three seems to somebody barely out of her twenties? His teeth will be falling out by the time he's out of school. Nevertheless, he's stark raving certain that he wants to be a psychiatrist and makes an appointment with the dean of the university's medical school to talk about his latest ambition. "All first-rate med schools reserve one or two slots for the waffling oddball like you," the dean tells him, "the humanist with an advanced degree who hasn't found his proper niche." *Waffling oddball*? Like it's an advantage? I want to *kill* this guy!

"It's not that I'm giving up my passion for literature," my husband tells me. "Think of Chekhov."

I'm trying to figure out how "Lady with the Pet Dog" fits into my life right now and am coming up empty.

"Chekhov liked to say that medicine was his wife and literature was his mistress."

"And where does that leave me?" I ask.

Over the summer my agent calls with the news that *Redbook* has bought my story "New Shoes." They're going to pay me $1,250! I can't believe it. I'm screaming with glee. We'll be able to pay off the credit card debt. I go jump on the bed so hard the frame nearly breaks. The story is about a young woman who has sacrificed to put her husband through medical school only to learn that he's decided he doesn't want to be a doctor after all. To celebrate his decision, he goes to a cheapo shoe store and buys a pair of pimp shoes—blue suede sling-back loafers with tassels and wedge heels—and struts around in them.

"It's not one of your best," my husband says when he finishes reading it. "I mean, the guy character is sort of a *joke*."

"Uh-huh."

"It's too ladies' magazine commercial for my taste."

"Well, somebody's got to be commercial in this family," I say. "Somebody's got to make money if somebody else wants to go to school for the rest of his life."

GRRRRIMSBORO

My father-in-law, the scissors baron, makes his son a job offer he's hard-pressed to refuse. Forget academia. Medical school is, after all, more school and more debt (not that my husband's ever been afraid of debt). Why not come home to Greensboro and family and the life of a tea cozy? When I was a teenager, growing up in Greensboro, Dr. Paul Bearer, the vampire host of a locally televised horror show, referred to the town as *Grrrrims*boro, bugging his eyes with terror.

"Come *grrrind* scissors at the scissors company," my father-in-law says, rattling the chains that bind. "Yes, come on home, son," my mother-in-law echoes, flexing all eight of her legs as she gears up to weave a web of apron strings. "It's high time you got your head out of the books and joined the *real* world."

"Stop! Wait!" I beg my husband. "Remember *The Magus*!"

The summer before we were married, when he was still living at home, one of his college English professors gave him a copy of John Fowles's novel to read. When his mother went snooping around his bedroom, she found the book, used her extraterrestrial radar to filch out a few sexually explicit passages and, horrified, summoned the baron. He brown-bagged *The Magus* like a sack of dog doo and promptly dropped it into the outdoor trash hole (they had custom-made buried trash cans in their yard, so abhorrent to them was the idea of filth).

But my husband seems to have forgotten this episode. He accepts his father's offer and tells me that I'm crying my shortsighted eyes out for nothing.

"I'm the one who's going to go to work for him, not you," he reminds me. "So what if he's ordered me to shave my mustache. Big deal."

"'Hurry my children, hurry. Lay down your life with dignity. Let's get gone. Let's get gone,'" I say, quoting the Reverend Jim Jones, who had recently persuaded nine hundred American cult members to drink poisonous Kool-Aid in an act of mass suicide at the People's Temple in Guyana.

"What's so great about a mustache anyway?"

"I *like* your mustache."

"It's just hair. It'll grow back."

"Not in *Grrrims*boro!"

"Greensboro's a nice place to settle down," he says. "What's wrong with Greensboro?" He's got the balmy voice of a Chamber of Commerce spokesperson. His eyes are as glazed as candied apples.

"That's the whole trouble," I say. "Greensboro's like the *black hole* of niceness. You probably only get one chance to escape its gravity, and if you go back, you'll be sucked down and disappeared into its mysterious nicey-niceness for life."

He gives me a pitying look. "Aren't you tired of being poor?"

"Yes and no."

"What's that supposed to mean?"

"What happens if, say, you're at work, and you drop a pair of scissors and you accidentally let fly some really bad cuss word?"

"That wouldn't happen. Dad doesn't allow cursing."

"How could you work for somebody like that?"

"I just won't curse."

"Next thing you know, you'll be joining him for a drink after work."

"Dad doesn't drink."

"'Hey, bartender! Can we have two shots of Kool-Aid over here?'"

There's no use talking to me when I'm in meltdown mode. He throws up his hands. "Sheesh! Go phone your mother or write a story or something."

"*Sheesh?*"

"I'm practicing," he says.

If only I had access to nuclear weapons. But. Wait a minute. I *do* have access. What about my *writing*? What about the old pen-is-mightier-than-the-sword routine?

Instead of writing a story, I sit right down and build the A-bomb letter, simple as pie-instein, to drop on my father-in-law. I'm so confident of my surprise attack, my persuasive logic, that it doesn't seem possible any clear-thinking person could counter me. I protest that by ordering his son to shave his mustache, the baron is denying him basic civil liberties. And isn't that illegal? And couldn't we probably *sue*?

He writes me back immediately, choppity-choppity, in curt, toothy pinking-shear prose, warning me that until his son agrees not only to shave off the offensive mustache but also whack his hippy hair down to clean-cut nubs, there *is* no job offer.

I keep telling myself it's not Greensboro's fault that my in-laws have built a scissors empire there and have been able to seduce all four of their college-educated children into working at the factory. One by one they all tried to get away, but the baron's force field was too mighty, his monetary compensations too alluring. And, at present, there are no teaching jobs in my husband's field except for a possible one-year appointment at Kenyon College in Ohio. I'd have to quit *my* teaching job if we left North Carolina. I comfort myself with the knowledge that Chapel Hill is a feasible one-hour commute from Greensboro. *I* can still have a life there. Besides, knowing my husband's history of dissatisfaction with one job after another, I suspect his stint at the scissors company won't last forever, so I take heart. In my mind we're still gypsies making camp.

We buy a lovely old four-square Edwardian house with a wide front porch. It's on Isabel Street in a downtown neighborhood around the corner from *my* parents who, compared to my dour in-laws, twirl around us like a couple of Tinkerbells.

The house has four bedrooms upstairs and a screened-in sleeping porch. On moving day my father tapes a sign he's made, written on a sheet torn from one of his prescription pads, to the door of the littlest bedroom: NURSERY. I scratch through the word and write STUDY.

"Aw, honey, why'd you go and do that?"

"Leave her alone," my mother chides him. "Don't pay any attention to him," she tells me. "Ignore him, just like you did in high school."

Some day I will write that I don't really know which gives me the most pleasure: the making of a pie or a metaphor. But right now I'm feeling prickly, defensive, a cornered brown wren. Moving back to Greensboro, my husband abandoning academia, the life of the mind, for a job grinding scissors because it pays better feels cowardly and weirdly opportunistic. There's a self-sabotaging logic to the choice, like taking the silk purse and turning it into a sow's ear. I can't help seeing the life of a professor as silky compared to the life of a scissors grinder, even if the scissors grinder is the one driving the spanking new car. Every mirror I pass, I look for signs, not of aging gray hairs, but of the creeping oatmeal plainness of a settled life, bunkered by material things. Can that woman be *me*, a woman wrapped cozily in the shawl of her hometown with her snugly jobbed scissors grinder? I miss the chancy artist's life I was living in Chapel Hill. Yes, we were a little raggedy, but on Sunday afternoons we hung out with other raggedies, listening to the Metropolitan Opera's live broadcast from Lincoln Center while learning to make a roux for communal shrimp gumbo, or dressing up all sparkly to go to some gay friend's coming-out party, or crowding into the Student Union to see the free flicks: Bergman's *Wild Strawberries*, films by Luis Buñuel, Werner Herzog, Lina Wertmuller, Francoise Truffaut, Stanley Kubrick, and Ken Russell, Hiroshi Teshigahara's haunting *Woman in the Dunes.* And, oh, the sublime combination of a rainy Saturday and the Humanities Room at Wilson Library, winning you away from the crass, clanging world and making you believe you had every advantage: the amber glow of desk lamps, the languid creaks of wooden chairs floating in the cave-cool sepia air like random notes played on violins, the whisper and whir of your soft-leaded number-two pencil, the scent of its woodsy exhaust as it goes speeding across fresh paper, the humid, sober breath of research and curiosity huffing from the card catalog, the velvetized shuffle of the dog-eared cards. Thumbing through them felt like holding hands with Knowledge its reclusive self. If you got hungry while you thumbed or wrote or read or daydreamed, you looked no further than the shelves around you: hundreds of thousands of books were waiting to be eaten.

In Greensboro we buy new wallpaper; we buy new rugs; we pay painters, electricians, and carpenters to upgrade the house. We buy a new car; we *buy* a cat—the first purebred cat we've ever owned, a little brown Burmese named Governor, Guv for short, who'll be hit by a car before he's full grown.

I'm writing stories that my agent quickly places in *McCall's* and *Ladies' Home Journal* and *Seventeen.* Meanwhile she keeps asking me about the novel I'm supposed to be writing, and I keep lying that it's coming along just fine. Well, the doodles in the margins are. I have written the first page about fifty times, trying to jump-start the thing. The problem seems to be with the main character's name: Savannah Sweethbriar Nightingale. What is *wrong* with me that I've come up with such a high-strung, sidesaddle-riding, gilded lily of a name? Does it have anything to do with my lavish new Greensboro life? I'll be damned if I'll let a frou-frou character named Savannah Sweetbriar Nightingale live past the opening chapter. First of all, she just has to be either an equestrian doomed to break her pearly neck during a fox hunt or a somnambulist wandering around in a diaphanous nightgown on a moonlit plantation where she's bound to fall into a swamp. Let's see if I can arrange such an accident.

Summer 1981, and I am riding around leafy, drowsy Greensboro, North Carolina, miles and miles and miles from sexy, circusy Chapel Hill where I used to teach, where

I used to have a writing life. Now I'm too fat to teach or write. Too fat, too Great With Child, and drunk with the power of another kind of Creation. Today I am riding shotgun in my writer friend Candy's car. It's a vintage Lincoln Continental convertible, a turquoise parade float, loaded with flashing chrome. The radio's turned up full volume, some moldy oldie from the grooveyard playing something like "Stoned Soul Picnic," helping to revivify the late 1960s, when we were *really* young. We plan to cruise around in this thing with the top down, our long hair blowing like capes behind us, until our youth runs totally out.

Candy is nine months pregnant, due any second, and I'm about five months gone. We're best friends and lucky to have planned our pregnancies to coincide so that we can be pioneers together, forging a trail through the wilderness of motherhood in tandem. But for the time being, traveling along in the Lincoln, we've hitched our wagons to a kind of gauzy Milky Way of nowness, where every precious premotherhood second feels as wildly blazing as a star. At a stoplight, some greasers in an old muscle car with a burbling muffler rev its engine, challenging. We will no longer be girls when we become mothers, that much we're pretty sure of, so when the light changes, Candy carpe diems the hell out of the Lincoln, and we leave the greasers star-gazing in our dust.

When I cleaned out my office, I was so certain I would not go back to teaching that I threw away all my notes. I tossed a load of books, too. Halfway to my due date, I've gained nearly forty pounds, but the fat feels divine. It seems to be feeding the sputtery fire in my brain, my teachery/writery self going up in flames so that a mother can rise from the ashes. I am wallowing in my expansion, not lamenting it, my heavy stomach like a trophy in my lap. Candy steers the Lincoln towards our favorite bakery where, since we can't drink champagne, we get trashed on chocolate chess tarts instead. Two bulbous pregnant writer girls, riding around in a convertible on an August afternoon, laughing, goofing, *not* writing, eating pastries with our fingers, dribbling crumbs down our shirtfronts. As far from our writing desks as we can be. Is that the warmth of the setting sun on my head? Or has my brain spontaneously combusted from such proximity to giddiness and burst like one of those sizzling sky-filling chrysanthemum fireworks, spraying radiance everywhere?

My baby's two weeks late. I was due on Thanksgiving and today is December 6, 1981. I've gained nearly sixty pounds, and the only clothes that fit me are tepees. Even my thumbs are pregnant. I have big pouty Elvis Presley lips, and something really weird is going on with my legs. They look like a cross between balloons and baguettes— they don't have ankles anymore; the feet attached to them resemble over-yeasted loaves of bread, still rising. I'm sliding around in a couple of baking pans, since my shoe size has puffed up from an 8 1/2 to a 10.

Daddy stops by every night on his way home from his office to check my edema by pressing my giant inflated calves. Lash them together, and I swear you could just raft me down a river. Daddy's worried. His fingerprints linger in my skin as if he's just pressed cookie dough. But I'm not worried because all the fat cells that couldn't fit elsewhere in my body have taken over my brain. They won't allow me to worry about anything, because, frankly (and this is them talking, not me, because I'm too fat to talk), it's too late for worry. I did this to myself, this pregnancy thing, so I'd better get used to feeling as blimpy and unproductive as a hog in a wallow. And once the baby is *here,* the fat cells tell me, I'm *still* going to want to eat a banana cream pie in one sitting, because why deprive myself just because I've given up my freedom and career to have a baby? If anything, I'll be hungrier than ever, because boredom does that to people, and once I have a baby tethered to me, my biggest outing will be waddling off to the grocery store. And guess what's at the grocery store: all the stuff for making more banana cream pies!

I think I've got *pre*-postpartum blues. Is that me lumbering past a mirror—or a grounded dirigible? Worst of all, I've been trying to finish my short story "Wearing Glasses" to send up to *Redbook* before the baby comes, and every time I sit down to work on it and prop my breadloafian feet in a chair to ease their rising, the fat cells start reminding me that there's too much to do before the baby comes to indulge myself. How can I waste my precious last days of nonbaby writing some stupid irrelevant story about an anguished teenager who has a crush on her English teacher? "Why not write a story about washing all those cotton diapers you insisted on buying?" the fat cells carp. "Of course we'd never suggest that you get off your lazy ass and actually *wash* them."

I think I am trying to write the stupid, irrelevant story because I already miss my girlhood, whiny as that might seem. I *don't* tell the fat cells because they love any opportunity to make me nostalgic, especially for food. But the closer I come to becoming a mother, the more inspired I feel to examine what made me a girl. As if conjuring it on the page will keep me from losing it altogether. And not losing it altogether seems of paramount importance if I am going to be a reflective adult. How can I be a good mother if I'm not reflective? How can I help my child grow up if I've forgotten how I did it? Perhaps filtering girlhood through the lens of hindsight, I'll surprise myself with the news that I would rather be here in the fat and now than back in the lithe and dreamy there and then. That *selective* girlhood is essentially what a wise woman hankers for, not the whole tumultuous package.

Something strange is happening, and I'm not sure it's all due to hormones. I'm beginning to think that here—at the eleventh hour—my muse is pregnant, too. I'm suddenly feeling this swollen craving to write.

That night for supper, I make a big pot of carrot soup, following a recipe from the *Moosewood Cookbook,* with about a pound of pureed cashew nuts in it. It is the most delicious stuff I ever ate. My fat cells are rocking out, swinging their partners, whooping it up to the timpani of the baby's thrusts and kicks. I eat like Goliath (again), and afterwards I can't get comfortable, can't get to sleep. It feels like I've swallowed our clothes dryer and it's filled with tumbling, thudding shoes.

I'm not surprised to wake up at 3:00 A.M. with a ferocious stomachache. Is it a stomachache or a roller coaster? Worse than a dryer, I've swallowed a *roller coaster* loaded with peaks and valleys and hairpin curves and all those screaming people.

"What's the matter?" my husband asks, fumbling for the light switch.

"Too much carrot soup. Maybe it will help me to sit up and burp."

"Try not to thrash around so much, I can't sleep."

Somehow we've both forgotten that the baby is two weeks late, but the baby hasn't. Soon we're at the hospital and checked into a labor room where I'm already hollering for a can opener to expedite the delivery. "It's *not* anything as benign as a baby!" I yell. "Don't you people get it? DO SOMETHING!"

When do you take a shower? That's the thing I can't figure out. I've been up three times during the night to nurse the baby, my beautiful, creamy, colicky boy, and of course I'm sleeping in. Then at 6:00 A.M. (that's daytime, isn't it?), I'm up and I'm feeding him again. Then we fall asleep and snooze until 8:00 and I feed him. Then he's fussy. Why is he fussy? He won't say. You can't leave a fussy baby while you scamper off to brush your teeth, let alone take a shower. You can hear the fussing, no matter how you try to insulate yourself, and the sound makes splinters in your heart and your brain. It's dictatorial: Hitler in baby form. Think of your life as a windshield, and you're cruising along admiring the view until you detect your baby's whimper, no louder at first than a little pebble pinging against you, bouncing off, leaving the teensiest scratch. But the scratch starts creeping. First it slinks into a sliver of line, then a slithering zigzag. It starts branching out, radiating, making a zithery wagon-wheel design and finally crazing into a blind of webbing that obliterates the view. You have no choice but to pull over before the whole windshield collapses or you run into a bridge abutment. You can't say, "Oh, that's just my baby going off again. Never you mind. Let him bleat for a while." Your whole life's about to wreck if you do. Besides, you're a Milk Dud on a short leash. If he cries, your nipples hear it and they cry back.

"Take a shower when *he*'s still there in the morning," my friend Candy suggests. She's referring to my husband who, it seems to me, has left the premises by 6:00 when my day starts. This can't be true, but that's how it feels, that he's shirked off our bedlam for the relative serenity of work. I smell remnants of a civilized world, drifting from

Savannah Sweetbriar Nightingale, somnambulist, wandering around in a diaphanous nightgown, right before she fell into the swamp.

the kitchen below where he drank coffee and read the paper and had his nipples fully dressed and to himself.

I go days without a shower, it seems. I grow stalactites of crud by the time I wash up. I've got skeins of Spanish moss dangling from my teeth.

"But it's worth it, isn't it?" Candy asks. Easy for her to say, as she zooms along on her novel. Secretly, I hate her. She's got a woman named Mary, sweet as Baby Jesus's mother, working for her five days a week, who not only cleans house but changes diapers and has supper cooked when Candy comes home from a tough day of writing. A tough day of writing: I should be so lucky. Give me *any* sort of writing day: lying on a bed of nails and suckling a child while I do it, writing by flashlight in a darkened storm cellar with only a laundry marker and a stack of clean diapers for paper while a cyclone gyrates overhead. All preferable to not peeping out a single word.

It marks the end of time as I once knew it, having a baby. The theory of relativity has gotten scrambled up and revised and folded into the theory of new relatives.

"But it's worth it," my mother-in-law says. It's not a question. And I say yes, grudgingly. What else can I say to her? When she holds the baby, her spiderliness completely vanishes, and she transforms into a chirpy house wren of happiness. What's more important, more thrilling than a new life? I'd be a monster if I said otherwise. But did Mozart think that way? Or Jackson Pollack? Or Gertrude Stein? Or D. H. Lawrence? Lawrence's wife, Frieda, abandoned her children to marry him. Where are the great women artists who sacrificed their families to make art? They're in the museum of the weird and the crazy and the early dead, like Sylvia Plath. Or they're considered monsters.

Is it okay to be a monster if you don't hurt anybody?

The baby's been screaming all day. He has an ear infection. Meanwhile, I've been watching the budding of scales on my legs, new ones breaking out and cladding me hourly (I'm beginning to clank when I walk). Where my fingers used to be, there are claws like yellow icicles. When I start to make supper, I light the gas stove simply by breathing some fire. I phone my mother. "It's not worth it," I tell her.

"Meet me at the front door. I'll be right over," she says in her calm, omniscient way.

Sylvia Plath would have made it if my mother had been hers.

But I do love my baby, I do. I do. Here and there I sneak a shower, brush my teeth, comb my snarly hair. I write a sentence or two, a paragraph, a chapter, the beginning of a new novel, *the* novel, as things turn out. If the baby can't stop me, then nobody can. I'm the Gingerbread Writer, I am, I am.

I return to the university to teach writing when Roderick is nine months old.

"What's the difference between snowmen and snowwomen?" Max asks me in the hall.

I shrug.

"Snowballs," he says gleefully and snickers.

"Hey," I say, "at the end of the day the balls melt, too, and somebody—most likely a woman—mops up the puddle."

He looks crestfallen. "You've changed," he says.

It's a little bit true. "I know my pain tolerance better," I tell Max.

On the days I drive over to Chapel Hill from Greensboro, I miss my little boy. He's perfectly cared for by one grandmother or another. But his moist fruity smell clings to my clothes, and, deprived of touching him, my hands feel a little bit parched and hungry.

I keep thinking of kissing his forehead, smooth as blank paper, his pudding-soft skin, his dark blue curious eyes as round with surprise as polka dots. He's like another country where I go to speak a juicier, more edible language.

"What are you writing these days?" a colleague asks.

I'm pleased to inform anyone who asks that the protagonist of my one-page stalled novel, Savannah Sweetbriar Nightingale of the pampered plantation life, is gone with the pen. I pushed her into a rice paddy because I knew she couldn't swim. I've started a new novel about a small-town girl named Pally Thompson. Her lack of pretension suits me.

So, I *am* still writing, but I've slowed down. There doesn't seem to be any good reason to hurry, and I'm resigned never to finish any novel I start. How could I? Not without giving up long, uninterrupted afternoons of watching sunlight travel the nursery walls. I stand over the crib, mesmerized. I can get lost in the whorls of Roderick's budding, pale cowlicks, the dusky colors of his sleeping eyelids. I hold his perfect, tiny hand and it gloms pinkly onto my own like a warm snowflake.

"Think my story needs more flashbacks?" a student asks me after class.

"Baby," I say.

"Excuse me?"

"Babybabybabybabybaby."

So, it's sometimes a dulling life and sometimes a thrilling one. Still life, with baby. Thrill life, with child. Now that I've gotten the hang of it, accepted my identity as Silly Putty in human form, parenthood isn't the bog I first felt. It *is* a liquid medium, but more like a choppy ocean, churning under a moonless sky. You learn to keep your head above water, and that's about all the control you have. You're treading water, holding your breath, going under, bobbing up in fits and starts of decent judgment. You keep afloat by buoys of tender instinct and intuition and a holler for help now and then. You do it all clumsily, luckily, but you do it: the biggest, most complicated dare of your life.

Meanwhile, my muse is getting really, really fat.

"One second I'm hovering above your head and the next thing I know—BOOM!" she says.

"Who's the father?"

"Don't make me laugh. We muses don't work that way."

"When's it due?"

She sighs. "Whenever you get serious and deliver."

"Boy or girl?"

"My intuition tells me that it's going to be a roller coaster," she says.

UPON FINISHING THE NOVEL

Ten

Summer of the Refrigerated Manuscript

Summer 1984—don't ask me what's going on in the world. George Orwell could be right, for all I know. I do recall that Ronald Reagan is president; I hear about Jane Fonda's workout videos; I know who Gloria Steinem is, but I don't have time to read her latest guide for the oppressed hausfrau: *Outrageous Acts and Everyday Rebellions.* If only I had the strength—or the anger. My brain's been sugar-plummed by motherhood. It's been twenty years since the Beatles appeared on Ed Sullivan and I thought of myself as a hipster. Babies and writing, that's all I'm scrambling to do. I've developed a theory that in order to get my writing done, I first had to make my life as impossibly hogtied as a Houdini stunt. I needed to be running out of both air and time in order to find some of either. Shackle my hands, blindfold me, ball-and-chain the muse, and I will figure out a way to loosen myself and write.

I've made so much progress on my novel that it's starting to seem valuable. Oh, but that's a risky way to think, especially when I can't explain the manuscript's worth to anybody except to say that if it were lost or stolen, I could never duplicate it. I'd rather vanish down a sewer hole and clamp one of those round, waffle-iron lids over myself than try to start this tome again from scratch. It's not just a hefty box of six hundred plus pages; there's all sorts of literary fallout you *don't* see floating over it—the shimmering afterimages of trial and error, ghosts of Wite-Out, snags and deliberations, self-doubt as snappish as mousetraps, slack-jawed moping, fifteen thousand cigarettes, at least that many pieces of chewed bubblegum, layers of plot digressions as itchy and unbearable as cable-knit sweaters in July unraveled and trashed, fear and loathing of the written word altogether, and Edvard Munch's *The Scream.*

I am typing this monster on an IBM Selectric II typewriter. There's *one* copy, no carbons. The novel's as singular as a new life and owed all due respect as such. But because it's one of a kind, the manuscript has taken on the insufferable demeanor of a tyrant on the verge of a temper tantrum. I'm a little bit scared of its power and way too much in its thrall. Deep down I realize that not making a Xerox is probably as stupid as arrogance, so I've started stashing the precious, awful, fussy thing in the freezer compartment of our refrigerator. In case of fire or theft.

"Who'd want to steal a bunch of typed-on pages?" my husband says, snickering. "A ream of blank paper maybe, but not paper that's already been *used.*"

"Do you have to put it that way? 'A bunch of typed-on pages?' It's called a novel."

"Come to think of it, probably nobody would steal *blank* paper either."

I know he's right, that I'm being irrational and paranoid. But just let him try spending years herding hundreds of thousands of wild and woolly words out of nowhere and gentling them into captivity, and he'll start believing in literary wranglers and poachers, too.

I miss teaching, but it was time to chuck something. You can't do it all—I don't care what the feminists say. I might as well have crawled down that sewer hole for all my lack of trendiness. You don't do pop culture anymore if you spend half your time shepherding small children and the other half bending over a manuscript as devotedly as a monk. I once heard a rueful Lee Smith declare that she totally missed the sixties because of having babies and throwing Tupperware parties.

During the last class I teach at UNC–Chapel Hill (in some delusional state of mind that I have anything of value to say to anybody), I'm reading a student's manuscript out loud, reading it cold, and out of the corner of my eye I glimpse two words galloping my way. How am I going to pronounce them once I arrive at them? They sure look French to me: this is what I'm thinking, as I enter the homestretch of the sentence where they appear like hurdles. I'm breezing along now, confident, juicing up my lips, curlicuing and frenchifying them and, when the two words arrive, I *think* I'm adequately prepared, and I say, "B*one* Jzho-*veee*!" With gusto. The way I imagine Colette or Simone de Beauvoir would say the phrase. For a second, there's only amazement hanging over my class like a blast, the debris of exclamation marks raining down.

"What did you just say?" one of the profoundly dumbfounded asks.

"My French is pretty bad."

"*It's not French!*" the students cry in unison.

OK, OK, so I needed somebody to inform me that Bon Jovi is a rock star.

I honestly thought it was a French term meaning "good

something." But when was the last time I listened to the radio? "I can honestly say that I wish I were cool, like y'all," I confess to the class. "But I'm not. It's not my time in history to be cool. I'm a mother, and mothers are *not* cool, unless you're talking about Grace Slick, the lead vocalist in Jefferson Airplane. She had a baby girl and named her god, little 'g.'"

"That's an urban legend," some smartass says. "She named the kid China. Besides, if you want to talk about cool mothers, Bon Jovi's was a Playboy Bunny *and* a United States Marine!"

"I just want you all to remember *one thing* from this class that was taught to you by a person who was so uncool she pronounced Bon Jovi in French. One thing, OK?"

"What is it?" some heavy-lidded, cool person asks, ratcheting up from his slouch.

"That I predict there will come a time when you won't be cool either. When you have children and are unable to tune in to the latest music because, frankly, either you won't have time for it or you won't be able to justify having more *noise* in your life for fear of sensory overload, remember how you laughed at me for my Bon Jovi faux pas. You'll be just as french-fried in the brain as I am. Whole years will blitz by while you, too, bliss out on Muppet songs."

They're all just looking at me, stunned with pity. What irrelevant nonsense am I babbling?

I have *two* boys now, twins the hard way, I sometimes say. Roderick—almost three—and Sam, almost fifteen months. There are reasons parents measure babies' ages in weeks and months. Time slows and thickens and crawls before it can toddle or run. A child *ekes* toward autonomy, and the more autonomous the child, the more liberated his caregivers. When my youngest son finally outgrows his crib, I will feel so gleeful about getting rid of the cagelike thing that when I can't find a screwdriver to disassemble it, I'll crack it apart like a bunch of kindling with my bare hands and javelin its pieces into the attic.

For the present I am the Mommy Bus, transporting them downstairs in the morning for breakfast, one boy per hip. Thank goodness I have two hips; heaven forbid that I would carry only one boy. Because, say I didn't *feel* like toting fifty pounds of kids down the stairs to the kitchen, the kid left behind would wail red alert, Moscow push-the-button-to-oblivion red, and it would incinerate the house, and the trees in the front yard would vaporize from the blast. This is my fear, as I stagger downstairs with my load. I worry that one of them will produce the wail that finally obliterates existence as we and all our neighbors know it.

Oh, the life I am leading in order to write my refrigerated novel. I schedule interviews with college girls who want to babysit. It's important to determine if they are psychos or not—one girl shows up in a car plastered with decals of skeletons. Turns out she's sweet as pie; the skeletons are tributes to the Grateful Dead, who are probably Bon Jovi's best pals.

One sitter—a tall, lush, dark-haired girl with a smile like Sophia Loren's—says, "You're not going shopping? You're not meeting friends for a movie? You're going *where*?"

"I'm going to my cramped, grubby, un-air-conditioned office to write," I say, "but, hey, it's a room of my own."

"You're paying me so that you can . . . *write*?" She's incredulous. She tries to stifle a laugh. "Pardon me, but that's crazy."

I shrug.

"Gosh," she says, "you couldn't get me to write anything when it's this hot, except a check for a new bikini."

Before I leased my little office, I had to peel the wailing kids off my legs like livid barnacles—they were big on separation anxiety. I'd bestow upon their cheeks the lipstick tattoos they were clamoring for, wave goodbye, charge outside, leap into my car, pray it would start, grieve for three seconds at the sight of their howling, steaming, crybaby faces pressed to the glass of the front door, drive around the block while the babysitter distracted and soothed them and my guilt abated, then park and slink back into the house via the basement where I'd set up writing for a couple of hours in the musty, lackluster dimness. Overhead my other life throbbed and thwunked its chaos. Good luck tuning it out. Fred Chappell once told me that when left to write at home with his young son, who was screaming to be set free from his playpen, he sprung the kid from captivity; then, lugging his typewriter, Fred crawled into the playpen himself to work. The arrangement made everyone happy.

My office is pure sanctuary. It's at the Sternberger Artists Center, on the second floor of an old mansion that once served as a children's hospital annex. My room measures about seven feet by eight. It doubles as a hall for the artist who rents the studio behind me and accesses her space through mine. I have a view of the broken concrete parking lot and the dented trash cans, the garage, a stunted orchard, and a mournful-looking German shepherd on a chain tied to a clothesline in somebody's backyard. Beyond lies the sketchy neighborhood. You can hear the booming PA system over at War Memorial Stadium some days, so I have to run my floor fan at high speed to drown it out. Every piece of paper in the office rattles and tries to lift off when I do this. I find some old bricks lying around outside the building, and I haul them upstairs to use for paperweights. The office comes furnished with a clunky, old, schoolteacher's desk and a sprung swivel chair with a lopsided seat. I build a bookcase with cinderblocks and boards. There's no air-conditioning, and this is North Carolina in July, when humidity is as thick as jam and sometimes breathing feels the same as drowning. Some days it's so hot that my typewriter cassette ribbons start melting. No joke, first thing I do when the writing's going well is kick off my shoes, strip down to my underwear, and type in the seminude. It's cooler. I've got a seashell ashtray, brimming with cig butts, and a quote I cut out of a calendar and pasted on my door, cheering me on: "From error to error one discovers the entire truth." Supposedly Sigmund Freud wrote it. But when I walk in that office, hard as I try and even if my brain's boiling like a cauldron, I feel less like an intellectual and more like a mechanic. I become somebody ultraphysical: a farmer, gymnast, carpenter, mason. I roll up the proverbial sleeves—well, actually I remove them altogether—and flex my muscles. I heave to and prepare to sweat.

My writer friend Candy has a fancy office down the hall. It's got air-conditioning, a rug, a refrigerator, a sprawling sofa, a closet, a photocopier, a telephone, and windows that look out on Summit Avenue and all the people making drug deals or shuffling along going nowhere fast or turning tricks or hobbling up the street to Mrs. Winner's for a chicken biscuit, which is where we writers often head for lunch ourselves. One thing I like about Candy is that in spite of her riches, she's comfortable slumming. Candy says she likes being on the Summit Avenue side of our building because it provides fascinating distractions. She can sit and watch the prostitutes and the destitutes and the occasional person of purpose ambling up and down the sidewalk all day, inspired by their untold mysteries. But I'm lucky to look down on the trash cans, she assures me. With no distractions, I'll get more writing done. Back in my sweltering little office, having refreshed myself in her air-conditioning, I look out on my potholed and bashed-up vista and count my blessings. My old, scabby 1973 Buick Estate Wagon is parked beside her vintage BMW, complete with red leather seats, that her husband gave her for her thirtieth birthday. The BMW has a vanity plate: ILUVBOOKS. Truth to tell, it makes my heart soar. I light another cigarette and park it on the seashell where it will burn slowly down as I engross myself in the task of writing a book I hope somebody will love one day.

My agent talked me into writing a novel. I'm much better suited for writing short stories, a genre V. S. Pritchett described in 1982 as "the glancing form of fiction that seems to be right for the nervousness and restlessness of modern life." Truthfully, I don't know how anybody writes a novel or what, exactly, a novel is. I know heaps more about its inexactness, the be*wilderness* of the process, the switchbacks, the sawtooth brambles that complicate the journey, and the constant childlike hope of finding buried treasure without a map. Because there is no map, and you think you ought to have one, you make guideposts for yourself. You divine them, actually, from books you are reading, from listening to people you deem wise and luminous, from superstitions, and sometimes from something as happenstance as a Chinese proverb you unroll from a fortune cookie. When your writing's going well, the world flickers with evidence of your progress, unveils auspicious symbols for your keen eye only. When you're stumped, the flashing light you were heading toward turns out not to be the aurora borealis after all, but a sputtering "No Vacancy" sign, because the world's too full of writers anyway. I've been learning to reconcile the tedious distance between setting out and arriving someplace worth the effort since childhood family trips in a claustrophobic car. "Daddy, how much further?" my brothers and I whined during the long, circuitous route from North Carolina to Mt. Vernon, Illinois, to visit our maternal grandparents. "How many more miles?"

"Eight hundred and twenty-nine," he'd answer us every time.

"Let's watch for Burma Shave signs," Mother suggested, and it helped. It gave us an illusion of purpose, distinguished us from the suitcases piled in the trunk. Otherwise we were squirmy hostages of Daddy's relentless plan to drive us to Illinois with as few stops as possible. He was as focused on ticking off the miles as if he were hauling time bombs or wildebeests about to gnaw through their restraints.

> *The Bearded Lady*
> *Tried a jar*
> *And now she is*
> *A Movie Star.*
> - Burma Shave

The signs, all snappy red and white, popped out of cornfields like Cracker Jack prizes.

Now, decades later, I'm the driver, only it's a novel not a car, and it's barely crawling. "How many more miles?" I ask myself. I am thirty-seven years old. How many more *years* till I get there?

If only I were able to post a rallying quote from Annie Dillard's *The Writing Life* above my typewriter: "The sensation of writing a book is the sensation of spinning, blinded by love and daring. It is the sensation of rearing and peering from the bent tip of a grassblade, looking for a route." But she hasn't inchwormed this marvelous book to completion yet; it won't be published until 1989.

Instead I've got a manifesto from Hemingway taped to my wall and booming at me all holy and austere: "[A] writer should be of as great probity and honesty as a priest of God; either he is honest or not, as a woman is either chaste or not, and after one piece of dishonest writing he is never the same again."

Beside it hangs a stern Shakespeare quote that reads: "I wasted time and now doth time waste me."

Plus I can't shake the memory of some dog-in-the-manger definition from Ambrose Bierce's *Devil's Dictionary:* "[Achievement is] the death of endeavor and the birth of disgust." So why finish anything?

Might as well add in a diet of moldy bread crusts and cups of rusty water, too, and just sit in my writing cell all bummed out till I rot.

The young heroine of my novel, Pally Thompson, lives with her mother in a turquoise trailer in tiny Orfax, North Carolina. It's 1961 and a boy she went to high school with (with whom she hardly spoke) has become a rock-and-roll sensation and written a risqué love song (banned on some Southern radio stations) that's climbed the charts to become a national hit. The title of the song is "Pally Thompson." The notoriety is wrecking Pally's life. Why did he do this? I am writing the novel to find out, and most days I'm completely stumped.

Some afternoons, it's a relief to go home to the bedlam. I plop the manuscript back in the freezer and start making supper while the boys and our cat, Jack, tumble around on the kitchen floor. "Smell Jack's tongue," I hear the older one tell his brother.

"Naw," the little one says.

I turn around and see that Roderick has wrestled the cat onto its back and pried its jaws open as if for a dental exam. "Smell," he says, leaning in for a bold whiff himself.

Sam tilts forward, takes a snort of cat breath, and makes a drama-king face.

"It smells *good*," his brother insists. "It smells like *okra*." Okra! And that's when I have to stop what I'm doing and drop down on my knees and smell Jack's tongue too. And Roderick's right. It smells like okra. I'd have never guessed.

I write the quote down on a magnetized pad that hangs on the fridge for just such occasions.

Another day they're playing in the den with their blocks. Earlier, we'd been driving somewhere when an old Peter, Paul, and Mary song came on the radio and I sang along with it. Now, as I'm making lunch, I hear the older one singing the song and the baby trying to hum along. When I call them for lunch, they don't hear me, they're still singing the song, and it's not until I look in on them that I see they've sprung Hammy from his hamster cage and set him spread-eagled and spinning on the record player turntable at 78 RPMs. Hammy's about to throw up; his eyes are totally boinged. What they're singing is what they think they heard: "The *hamster*, my friend, is blowin' in the wind, the *hamster* is blowin' in the wind."

After I rescue the hamster, I note their malapropism on the kitchen pad. too. I write down everything. Writing down the tiny stuff is the writer's equivalent of bronzing baby shoes. "The writer is sentenced to a lifetime of observations . . . a lifetime of sentences," is how Fred Chappell describes what I'm doing. And it's true, because I seem to have no choice years later but to write down Sam's declaration that he smelled snakes in the woods and the snakes smelled "jumbly." "Can a spider get caught in its own web?" he will ask me when he's older. "Which would you rather be: good and dead or bad and alive?" "Would a person survive longer if he had nothing to eat or if he ate a little bit of himself every day?"

"One of the most wearying things about the discipline," Fred says of writing, is that "there is no escape from it." And not only are you writing down what seems of interest to you or pertinent to some discovery, but you are pondering its phrasing, too, trying to measure its most artful arrangement, like a jeweler arranging stones in a crown. You're also trying to discern the answer with which you suspect every question is imbued. Even if you don't write down the answers.

It's better not to write down the answers. Write down the puzzlements instead; make yourself as lost as you dare. Think inside out; be a worm spiraling inside an apple, blind but fat. Tendril your mind. Seek like a trumpet vine, not a tight little cabbage.

One sticky, superheated August afternoon, I write the final sentence of my book. Which comes first, the joy on my face or that grand finale word? You'd think I might have seen it coming, but, no, it ambushes me. I sit staring at it a while. Then I say it out loud. My book ends with the word *smile.*

How can you be sure you've finished a book if you've never finished one before?

It's muggy hot. A dense, overcast sky churns like curds of iron. The wind smells wet. OK, I think, as I drive home from my office, go ahead and rain on my parade, storm the storm of the century and who cares? *I've got my book.*

I'm thinking this, not saying it aloud, not even whispering it. Even whispering would be perilous. I know this. Every sane writer knows this. Hubris is the precursor of nothingness—that's what lots of us hardscrabble writers believe. All art—triumphant or not—is absolutely precarious. *I've got my book.*

Rain splats big and messy as dropped eggs as I dart from my car into the house. It's the lightning I hate. I'm terrified by it, ever since about 1954 when, during a ferocious thunderstorm, Mother made us all crouch in the hallway of our blacked-out house where pink electricity spidered out of wall sockets and built sizzling webs of electrocution up and down the gloomy air.

Now lightning crazes every which way overhead followed by landslides of thunder. The sky has an eerie furnace glow, and the wind is suddenly too still, like a bully pretending to be good. I know the signs that presage a really bad storm, but I say let it rage! *I've got my book.*

My husband's home from work early, the babysitter dismissed. He's talking on the phone while the children totter around him. I scoop them up and nuzzle them. I touch my forehead to each of theirs in turn and beam my joy: *I've got my book. It's done. You get to have your love slave back.*

My husband hangs up the phone, frowning. "Your mom says a tornado's touched down. Better get everybody into the basement."

Quickly we gather blankets, a radio, a flashlight, and, each of us carrying a child, we descend into the murky netherworld of the house. It's not always a dry basement, but this time it is. We spread the blankets on dusty concrete and hunker down. The children think we're going to have a picnic in the dark. Now what? The radio doesn't deliver a speck of information about the storm, just rock and roll. Seems like the rest of the world has moved on to less-endangered times. I hear the wild rain and the wind beating like cannibal drums, but all the stations are playing Billy Joel.

There's a lull in our panic, and that's when I remember. *I DON'T have my book.* In my haste to vacate the car, I left the thing in the backseat. My *only* copy. My singular tyrannical novel—and, boy, is it furious. I can hear it slamming and slapping its pages against the car's interior, trying to paper-cut its way through to safety.

Oh my God. I left my novel in the car.

"Did you say something? It looked like your lips were moving," my husband says.

"My novel. I left it in the car," I say like a wall-eyed zombie.

He shrugs. How can he shrug if he's seen *The Wizard of Oz*? Doesn't he realize that once the tornado eggbeaters through our neighborhood, the car will end up lassoed around some tree, smashed, the contents jettisoned? My scrambled-up novel will be dropping its pages like paper rain all over the southeastern United States.

"My novel," I repeat. "My novel's *dying* out there."

He's fiddling with the dial on the radio, trying to get a weather update. The children are bored, already starting to pick at one another. It's raining nails and daggers outside. The wind's blowing so hard that the basement windowpanes seem to flutter and flip in their mullions like decks of shuffling cards.

"My novel . . ."

"Well, don't look at me," he says. The dirty rotten coward.

I peel away from our protected huddle, charge up the stairs, race through the foyer, and blast out the front door. I dive into the shards of rain because there simply is no choice, no otherwise. The tornado's breathing its dragon breath on some other street, but I don't know this. All I know is that any second, as I race toward the car, I might get swept up and shish-kebabbed on a telephone pole.

It's raining so hard that my clothes feel shredded, my hair uprooted. The trees are roaring. The sky's a black lagoon. Leaves blown from the holly bushes puncture me like darts. I am maneuvering toward the car by clutching branches, going hand-over-hand as if traversing monkey bars blown sideways. *The car keys. I forgot the car keys!*

I don't know which is louder, my heart or the rain. By the time I've inched backward to the house, dug up the keys, and slunk out to the car so that the lightning can't see me, the storm's over. The sky is yellowing in the west; our street unfurls sashes of steam; birds chirp their forgiving syrupy notes, and, way off, the thunder sounds as chuckly as somebody shooting billiards. I lift the spotlessly dry manuscript from the backseat, cradle it, and hasten it inside. Damn, the thing looks miffed and pouty. But before I nestle it back into the freezer I kiss it nearly to smithereens.

Eleven

The Happiest of Endings

Doesn't matter if it turns out you could be the next great voice in American Letters—Ernestine Hemingway or Wilhelmina Faulkner—you've got to get past The Agent. If she hates the novel, she won't be able to convince a single editor otherwise. My agent knows I've typed the damn thing from start to finish five solid times, so she wouldn't dare get picky, would she? Having recently swaddled my infant manuscript and placed it in her care, I still believe in agents as art-loving humanitarians, not fire-breathing monsters who'd just as soon gnash a manuscript as waste their precious time reading it. I've met Ginger, lunched with her, observed her dainty table manners—she does not *eat* like Godzilla—and traded comradely southernisms with her. I can't help thinking of her as chicken soup in businesswoman form. I'd bet my right index finger (the Jane Fonda of my typewriter workouts) that Ginger's a tremulous antennae person, alert as a cattail spearing from a still pond waiting to register the slightest disturbance:

somebody skipping a rock—or a novel—across the pristine surface of possibilities. I am beholden to her. From the moment I submit my book, she is *right* and I am wrong. I work for her, not the other way around: this is the level of my gratitude and supplication.

On a late August afternoon the phone rings. I'm in the downstairs den, getting the children and myself all prepped for *Mr. Rogers.* There are two slim windows in the den that face west. The sun is streaming through the blinds in such a way that I see how dusty they are, *furred* with dust actually. Mink blinds. Dang, I'm such a *slob,* is what I'm thinking. A blizzard of dust motes paisley the air between the ringing phone and me. My mind has probably latched on to wondering what's *wrong* with me that my housekeeping skills are nil, and *why* have I put off until the eleventh hour what I'm going to make for dinner, and *how* am I going to kill the hour between *Mr. Rogers* and feeding everybody without dying of boredom or restlessness or a sense of my ineptitude as a domesticated human being, much less a writer. Here's an idea: maybe I should dust! Civilization was probably built on dusting. But part of me is wondering what would happen if I went outside and climbed a tree instead. It would be fun to climb a tree again, shoeless, no props, ropes, or ladders. Inside the topmost limbs, I'd be out of reach—except for, say, birds and ants. You've got to be out of reach if you want to *think.* Just *think.* I've recently read an essay by the Canadian writer Robertson Davies who declares how difficult it is to find one hour a day to simply process your day, reflect, mull, dumb down, whatever your brain likes to do on its time off. Everybody you know, Davies writes, will try to claim or obliterate that hour.

But for now, forget thinking: my phone is ringing and I scurry to answer it. Stimulus/response. "Hello? You rang?"

It's Ginger Barber, my agent, calling from New York.

Always, *always,* the sound of an editor or an agent calling me from New York is the sound of champagne pouring and Fred Astaire tap dancing to "Puttin' on the Ritz."

"I just called to say that I read The Novel in one solid whoosh and thanks a lot, you ruined my night."

"Your night? How? What did I *do*?" I wouldn't ruin her night for anything on earth. Oh, stab me in the heart with a poison pen should I be such a benighted dumbling!

"I loved your book *so* much," says the Almighty She, "that I stayed up till *dawn* reading it. Then the next day, *dead on my feet,* I had to give a *dinner party.*"

"You *did*?" I don't know what I'm responding to, that she loved my novel or that she had to give a dinner party without having slept. My brain's doing the roller coaster thing of careening around long curves of the ridiculous and swooping down silvery hills of the sublime. The Rolodex of my multiple personalities is shuffling like a deck of cards. Do I sound grateful or flabbergasted? Incredulous? Apologetic? Apoplectic or serene? Forget serene. The serene gene got omitted from my DNA.

"You *LOVED* it?" I'm definitely apoplectic.

"A wonder I got the meal on the table, and it's *all* your fault. I told my guests so. It's Marianne's fault. 'Who's that?' they asked."

"YOU LOVED THE BOOK?"

"I sent copies of the manuscript out this afternoon to Simon and Schuster, Putnam, Scribner's, and Random House."

To my ear it sounds like the Mount Rushmore of publishers.

"You're on your way, girl," Ginger says. "Congratulations. Time to uncork some bubbly."

Generic Editor

Simon and Shuster turn the novel down flat. So does Putnam. Scribner's and Random House send polite rejection notes that Ginger shares with me. "Not to worry," she says. *Yeah, right.* But I comfort myself knowing that Dr. Seuss's first book, *And to Think That I Saw It on Mulberry Street,* got rejected by dozens of publishing houses before it found a happy home.

I try not to fret about what's going on in New York, but of course I do. I imagine editor after editor reading my book, their guffaws of derision blending into a massive chorus of rejection. Some of them are probably going blind or crazy, others brain-dead, plowing through my corny hee-haw prose. They're phoning up their editor friends to warn them away: "Don't even read the first page! It's like sticking your brain in quicksand!" "Worse!" screeches another: "It's like trying to harvest a cornfield the size of Iowa—with your eyes!"

To subdue such paranoia, it actually helps to have humility, and I've got tons of it ever since I decided to turn pro at failure. To be a pro at failure, you can't fear it any more than you fear any force of nature that you fear mostly in the abstract because how often are we really attacked by grizzly bears or slammed by an avalanche? I've learned to think of failure as a fault line in my confidence, but not the fatal earthquake; it can be a knock-down-drag-out wave but not the tsunami eraser.

To achieve this state of failure Nirvana, you have to have been really *bad* at something in your life, accepted that you were never going to get any better no matter how you struggled, resigned yourself to your ineptitude, and moved on. My list of failures includes cheerleading, swan dives, changing a flat tire, piano, ballet, plumbing repairs, rowing a boat with two oars, maintaining beautiful fingernails, punctuality, writing poetry, reading *Moby-Dick*, Lamaze, my mother's recipe for "never fail"—ha!—caramel icing. All tip of the iceberg, compared to my continent-sized failure at math. My being savvy about publishing falls into the category of my lacking expertise, a prerequisite for failure that I'm hoping to circumvent entirely by turning over my manuscript to a professional intermediary: the agent. It's like contracting with a real estate broker, except it's a novel she's bargaining for, not a habitat. Although, a novel *is* its writer's dwelling place until the writer finishes it. You make a kind of home in a pile of pages and hope somebody will eventually admire how you furnished and decorated it.

Thumbelina's skinny sister

Most people of my generation remember exactly where they were and what they were doing when President Kennedy was shot. I was at Grimsley High School, Greensboro, North Carolina, sitting in skinny, young, brilliant Miss Moore's algebra II class. Miss Moore was so comfortable with algebra that she sort of yodeled it. She'd just handed back tests, and I'd made a fifty and was already sobbing when the principal came on the intercom and announced that the president was dead.

Algebra was completely indecipherable to me. To this day, I can read the Sanskrit of earthworms but not a quadratic equation. Even with Miss Moore's patient tutoring, I was doomed to make Ds and Fs. Cs were occasions for jubilation. I'd learned to give up on algebra and not fight my failure because my brain lacked both the armor and the passion for fighting. It was not a matter of simply buckling down. It was a matter of cerebral wiring and recognizing that—unlike Sylvia McSween who sat across from me in creative writing class and appeared to be as splendid a writer as she was a mathematician—it was inhuman to be equally good in all things. I suspected that Sylvia—a great icy beauty on top of all her academic success—was likely an alien. Believing this was one of the reasons I was able to drag myself to school each morning to compete with her and others like her. That she made superlative grades in every subject, got elected to the Homecoming Court and nominated for May Queen, and went steady with tall, handsome Bertram Lord, an intellectual nobody jeered because he also played varsity basketball and drove a yellow Corvair convertible—well, it was too lucky. That much success in high school pointed to an inevitable reversal of fortune, postgraduation, didn't it? Unless, before life on Earth got dicey, Sylvia's true people called her home to Uranus.

"You have . . ." she once said to me in creative writing class, "very beautiful . . . hands."

"Oh? Huh? You think? Gee."

"They're so expressive, graceful," she said, "like . . . wands."

I looked at my bony, neglected hands, as if for the first time. Wands were actually *sticks*. Hmmmm. I observed the ragged cuticles and bitten-down nails and a bulging writer's callus on the right middle finger. That finger looked like Thumbelina's skinnier hunchbacked sister. My writer's callus was not a speck beautiful (it was a *deformity*), but whenever it lumpily braced a pencil, my concentration turned aerodynamic and I experienced liftoff. Had Sylvia's eye spotted some essence of latent sorcery in my hands? Or was she making idle chitchat? It's impossible to make *idle* chitchat with a writer, Sylvia! For a writer, even the lamest of words (and compliments) is brimming with potential and aiming to leap tall buildings at a single bound and do *anything* but stay idle.

She and I both made A's in creative writing class, but her remark about my hands had metaphoric weight. It helped me to differentiate my A from hers. Hers was the golden trophy A of a reliably solid performance; my A had been conjured out of thin air—a shaky, amateur magician's trick, like a bird fluffed awkwardly from a squashed top hat and struggling a little to fly. It was possibly an A—and I have given such A's myself—for something the teacher didn't feel qualified to measure, some novelty that made her think less of a trophy than perhaps an old tarnished lamp needing rubbing, a glass slipper with a crack in its heel. Less a grade, perhaps, than a vote for my promise, it was an A for the wobbly excellence that could never get me into Harvard, but it was by hook or by crook uniquely mine.

Ginger's steerage of my book after its delivery to her is the steerage of a superior mathematician—or strategist. I've let go of six hundred and something pages. It's just a number, after all.

Meanwhile, my four-year-old son seems to have fallen in love with the English language overnight, speaking incantations of euphonic new polysyllabic words: "sweet patootie," "rhododendron," "sockeroonie," "stethoscope." I laugh at him and applaud. We seem to be racing back and forth to one another over this bridge of word worship that he has built. Every word he recites is a juicy spoonful of poem. My husband teaches him Yeats's "Song of Wandering Angus," all five stanzas of the eighteenth-century hymn, "Our God, Our Help in Ages Past," and verses from Coleridge's "Kubla Khan" as well. How strange to hear a toddler with a face like a peony piping Coleridge, glorying in the delectable tropes and tra-lah-lahs of sound. Listening, I'm reminded how it all begins, this writing life: with a seesawing attraction to sounds you can lean into, rhythms that lilt and *mean*. There's an addiction first to lullabye, then perhaps to a riff of melodious nonsense, the potent sensation of words as arrows and charms. "In Xanadu did Kubla Khan a stately pleasure dome decree," my little one recites. "And there were gardens bright with sinuous rills / where blossomed many an incense bearing tree."

I finish an autobiographical story called "Putting the Babies to Bed" and send it to my agent, but nobody wants it. The editors of the women's magazines that have published my other stories find this one too blunt, too chock-full of grit to publish. Now, along with my faith in my writing, it seems I've misplaced my sense of humor and that my stories about motherhood have turned cranky. Why don't I write about my son's jubilant new vocabulary instead of him trying to destroy something: chopping off the cat's whiskers with scissors or catapulting the hamster with a homemade slingshot? He'd much rather be playing Ninja Turtle wars and slinging nunchakus at his brother than learning new poems. I write in my diary that my children's "boyishness—love of weaponry and battle games—bores me *utterly*. To the extent that my mind goes blank at the thought of how to entertain them. I tire of innovations that they don't appreciate. Sometimes I feel that I can barely share my imagination with them—as if it is a precious commodity that will get used up, or worse, wasted."

It's a complicated time. The sort of time that makes you wonder how anybody living an intensely domesticated life musters the resolve and focus, much less the hours, to peel away from the fray and write *anything*. A grocery list that makes sense would be nice. These days even the wallpaper's making me jumpy, and I can't listen to music while the kids are shrieking around. It's the *busyness* of everything, the interruptions, life as pileups of scurry, jolt, boom, screech, sob. I try to explain to my husband when he comes home from work, disappointed that Mozart isn't playing, why I'm not whistling as I work.

"Music's just more noise."

"Not *Mozart*!"

"But the wallpaper's too noisy for me to hear Mozart," I say. "I want to strip it all off. I want to paint every room plain. I want to throw away all the furniture and doodads. The house is too stuffed with stuff. It's all yammering and ticking, and I can't *think*."

He just gawks at me as if there's a tangle of coat hangers where a wife once stood. My black heart shrinks to the size of a pellet, a dot of buckshot, a licorice seed. A heart nobody wants.

It's like molting, getting rid of this funk, my sense of impending rejection and good-for-nothingness. I keep trying to write my way out of this thin, thin skin of mine, starting new short stories, wadding them up, starting another while I wait to see if the novel sells. My ears are constantly twitching towards the telephone, anticipating the ringing that will herald the sale of my book and change my life for the better. I didn't used to be a writer, and I was plentifully okay with that, wasn't I? I can't remember if I was okay or not because I have been a writer since I was six years old.

When the babysitter arrives, I trundle off to my little hamster wheel of an office to do the only thing I know to do that keeps me out of trouble, keeps me oddly sane and bright, heedless of insult, despair, dread, injustice, and stalled or wasted time. I've finally concluded that whether anybody buys my novel and stories or not, writing them makes me more vivid. "The artistic wager—the commitment to devote ever-lengthening years of one's life, say to the production of a novel—is manifestly unreasonable," the writer Mark Salzman explains in a *New Yorker* article about his publishing woes. "I take it on faith that art is worthwhile. I go on because I believe it's the right thing to do, not because I know it is." Amen.

I drive the rusty old lumbering Buick Estate Wagon we bought for four hundred dollars into the Sternberger Artist Center parking lot, where I hit all the potholes. The car shrieks ouch from every one of its leaky shock absorbers. The air conditioner is broken; the scratchy radio only picks up an occasional punitive blast of Oral Roberts; the back window is frozen at half-mast; the brown upholstery wears the sticky sheen of drink spillages and baby drool; the rear seat is littered with toys, teething rings, crayons, sipper cups, pacifiers, and—oops—there's Dr. Pinky, my

youngest son's little drag-along comforter. I do a U-turn, speed straight home, where, sure enough, the babysitter has been tearing up the house searching for the blanket while Sam howls. Nothing makes him any happier than to collapse on Dr. Pinky, sniffing its delicious grime, feathering the tip of his nose with its pink ruffles, snorting comfort. Once blanket and boy are blissfully reunited, I return to the office, hit all the potholes again, park the wheezy car under a tree and sit a while, *just sit,* soothed by the wind-jostled frill of leaves overhead, sniffing their ruffles, too.

Call me crazy, but it's not about the publishing, it's about the writing, the zoom and the bloom of it, "the gardens bright." By the time I leave the car and climb the stairs to the office and ease myself into the chair and turn on the rumbly IBM Selectric and settle back for a sweeping gaze of the fresh blank page that I've scrolled into the carriage, my brain's humming. A page of new writing seems to defy the science maxim I was taught in seventh grade: matter can neither be fully created nor destroyed. Well, there it is! The new matter of words, whether they matter or not, mined from the twinkling cave of my own head, fool's gold or not, and dumped out on the page.

I'm drawn to the blank page the way the wilderness explorer, having lost his compass, is drawn towards a clearing where he might once again look up, past the savage tangle of trees, towards a black sky pontificating with stars. For me, writing's not so much about the messy, meandering cavalcade of invention as it is about finding a clear path that leads somewhere, navigating the steep pitches and underbrush of thought and staying on course. Mark Salzman, who is also a cellist, compares the strategies of writers and musicians. He says,

For me art and music are alike in that they are about creating dissonance and then feeling compelled from within to resolve it. Bach literally could not leave a dissonant harmony unresolved. In ordinary life we face dissonances every day that we can't resolve . . . but when we write or listen to music or read or play an instrument, we relive the experience of making the journey from chaos to order, and that feeds us, reminds us, heartens us,

gives us courage to face all the journeys where there is no such
promise. And that's why Bach's suites are stories, too.

So there I sit in my little office, waiting not for a telephone
call, but for the words, the music, to start. My hand hovers
above the keyboard like a dowser's wand. I think it's
finally just about holding your breath and waiting for
some irresistible summons. Your tentative first words, the
ones you won't throw away, plink down as lonesome and
unlikely as an astronaut's footprints in moon dust. You're
high now, apart from all things ordinary. Lest you get too
breezy, there's punctuation to heed at the end of your first
sentence. Now what? The next sentence is waiting for you
to write it. Then another and one after that, which begs a
question only the sentence that follows can answer. You've
got the answer. And on and on you go.

When the telephone rings in the hallway outside my
door, I'm orbiting elsewhere. Another tenant answers it,
and dimly I hear her knocking on my door. "It's your
babysitter," she calls. "She says it's urgent."

Crashing hard, fearing that one of the children has
gotten hurt, I go flying to answer.

"Your agent phoned," the babysitter says. "I couldn't
find your office number to give her and she was in a huge
hurry. Sorry, Mrs. G., but it's a zoo over here. She says it's
wonderful news. She says to call her before six so she can
tell you everything. Got to hang up, one of them is trying
to bite the head off GI Joe!"

It's quarter till six. The children are okay. Nobody's hurt.
I'm not on my way to meet the ambulance at the hospital.
I'm on my way to get good news. After thirty-one years of
writing, I'm going to be a writer holding my own book. I'd
call New York from my office, but our communal phone

has no access to long-distance service. This is happening in 1984, the Pleistocene era before cell phones.

I leap down the stairs four at a time, gazelle across the parking lot, wrench open the car door—it would be easier to break into a vault—and jump in. I twist the key, and the motor cranks; I slam the automatic gear shift into reverse and do *not* go. It's a longtime intermittent problem with the transmission. The motor sometimes has to idle for about ten minutes before you can grind into reverse and back the hulk up. I can't go forward because three inches from the front bumper sways a grove of trees. So there I sit, furious and laughing and stuck. Waiting to go backwards before I can go forward. I think that's probably every writer's story. "Come *on*, you old dumpster!" I yell at the car, but it takes its sweet time engaging, my low-down chariot. When it finally lurches backwards, we skim over the parking lot potholes like skaters on ice. As we approach Summit Avenue, from secret side panels the Buick unfolds a pair of sail-sized wings, luminous as a dragonfly's, and we are suddenly airborne, rising over the traffic and floating low over green cumulus florets of trees, the ticklish jabs of telephone poles and rooftops, a water tower, a bobbing kite, a colorful escort of songbirds and runaway balloons. We circle once over the Sternberger Center, where through the window of my office I glimpse the novel's paper tower of five chunky drafts, piled one atop the other, three thousand pages high. I blow them a kiss, never imagining that two more drafts will join them once the editor who buys it has stopped praising the book and we've dug into line editing a hundred pages out. But for now, in the pearly loop-the-loop of triumph, flying high, at the summit of my long creative haul, I can't imagine writing a happier ending than the one that you are reading.

It's as good a mirage of a finish line as any, this laughing place of soaring satisfaction and basking in voilà. THE END, and let the presses roll, inklings of permanence giving way to ink and whatever follows, in life and in art. Fare-thee-well and hang on tight and good luck to writers, one and all.

Twelve

Ever After

Bobby Rex's Greatest Hit is published in October 1986, and my exuberant editor, Susan Leon, wires me a congratulatory telegram and signs it "Bobby Rex." I send her flowers and sign the card "Bobby Rex." *Ooooh, Bobby Rex!* We are such groupies. Due to her difficult pregnancy and the premature birth of her daughter, the book's publication has been delayed about nine months. In the cheerful aftermath of a safely delivered and healthy baby, she jokes about the postponement. Isn't it hilarious how somebody else's child can waylay your career? Ha-ha, we laugh, the irony! I could have had a couple more babies myself in the time it's taken to incubate this book from start to finish, I tell her. Ha-ha.

My husband has left his father's business and started his own rival scissors company by the time *Bobby Rex* gets reviewed by the *New York Times* in mid-December. I'm at his new office, numbly unpacking and inspecting boxes of scissors he's imported from Japan, when my agent

calls to tell me that I've gotten a review in the only place that matters. "It's a miracle!" she crows. "No one has ever heard of you or owes you any favors. You, a nobody writer with zero connections, reviewed in the *Times*! Start genuflecting, girl!"

"Would you mind reading it again?" I ask. Gosh, why I am still using that smarmy Little Match Girl voice with her? She probably likes me better, now that I've gotten a decent review. The one in *Glamour* wasn't so hot. That critic accused me of telling the wrong girl's story. She wrote that my teenage narrator was a goody-goody, and that the wild, promiscuous girl who got into bathroom brawls and had sex with twin redneck brothers that led to pregnancy (which brother was the father?) was the character she liked the best.

Ginger reads the review again to me. "'By turns hilarious, wry, maddeningly digressive, meditative, and almost rhapsodically lyrical . . . spangled with brilliant, exact images.'"

"What was that part about the novel being 'maddeningly digressive?'"

"It's just another way of saying that you're a Southern writer," Ginger says.

"Damn."

"Don't worry about it."

"Well, I wouldn't go out and buy a 'maddeningly digressive' book on purpose, would you? It's not exactly an endorsement."

"Who called?" my husband asks after I hang up.

"I got a nice review in the *Times*," I tell him. But I hear my voice tooting its horn a couple of octaves lower than usual. It's not the 'maddeningly digressive' comment that's gnawing at me. It's my husband's sagging, woebegone face. Sympathetically I feel my shoulders slump to match his posture, and I dial my brightness back a notch or two. His business isn't going well. I sense him hankering mightily to be a literary contender himself (he's got a flashy vocabulary, a Ph.D. in literature, and credibility as a local book reviewer). If he put his mind to it, he could write a book so brilliant he'd be hailed as Philip Roth's Waspish counterpart. In fact, there's absolutely no reason why he can't write a great novel—except that he doesn't.

He claims that he wants to pile up some money before he retires to the life of the mind, that the scissors company is a means to an end of financial mediocrity. He's fallen out with his father, cashed in his retirement, and second-mortgaged our house to finance the venture. He'd been so depressed working for his father that he bought a BMW to cheer himself up. Only now he's got to bust ass even harder in order to make the monthly car payments on top of paying our other bills. I've joined him today at the office to try to help, but I'm as grim as a troll. From the looks of the pathetic orders, it might be easier for us to attempt filling up the Grand Canyon with dollar bills than to pay off our debts.

In the rocky marital landscape of for better or worse, this is definitely worse. It's worst worse. I resent spending my precious time stuck doing a job I never applied for. Yes, I am a bad, bad sport. Yes, I'm failing some ultimate test of long-suffering wifedom. Inside me, where once beat a heart as soft and pliant as a cotton boll, a weevil lurks. But with both kids finally in school, I've got time for writing without hiring sitters (we can't afford sitters anymore). And now that I've got time for writing, to squander it packing scissors feels like muse abuse. I'm sitting at the cardboard-colored work table, staring at the cardboard-colored wall, shuffling my going-nowhere feet against the pebble-hard cardboard-colored carpet, flipping through a stack of invoices about a thick as one sheet of single-ply toilet paper, packing up the orders for the UPS guy. And why does it have to be scissors we're handling? Why couldn't it be something edible or fuzzy or adorable? I *hate* scissors, their steely aura of pragmatism, their smug posturing as necessities, their masquerade of singular pristine domestic purpose when everybody knows they can double as weapons. Closed up, their blades look as prim as steeples; opened and chomping, they have the vicious appetite of alligators.

Wait a minute. Do I understand scissors so well because I work with them? Or because I'm kindred, appearing to be a docile helpmate but dying to cut myself loose. Am I an alligator in church clothes, too? This is *not* a healthy way to view myself, but that's how I start thinking when I'm required to be in proximity with a pile of scissors on a day I want to be celebrating my writing life. I'm vowing never to use a pair of them again. I'll use a hacksaw or fingernail clippers or my big sharp teeth and claws if I want to cut or rip into things.

"You're sneering," my husband says.

"Nope. That was a yawn."

"Hey, you just got reviewed in the *New York Times*. Lighten up. What's the problem?"

It's strange to feel sparkly and plain at the same time. A gilded potato. Praised by an important book review, I am momentarily transcendent. But where am I going to fly? Potatoes don't fly; they aspire, after a hard day's work, to be couched. A root vegetable like a potato niches itself in cardboard-colored activities like boxing up scissors for shipment and mailing invoices. Then the lowly tuber tumbles home to cook supper, wash dishes, bathe two squirmy, bickering little spuds, and snug them into bed. When her husband sequesters himself in his study after dinner, paging through notes for his own embryonic novel, doesn't she owe him sanctuary? Because, if publishing a book can happen to an old half-baked Mrs. Potatohead, hasn't Professor Potatohead got at least triple the chance?

Later, in this land of ups and downs, just as silence settles upon the house, the pleasantries of rest and contemplation beckoning, I hear the agitated prance of

Potatoes Don't FLY

little feet on tiptoes. As if polka dots could trot. Then both children burst from their room, howling. They've gotten hold of a packet of itching powder and dared each other to rub it all over themselves. They blur into fits of twitching, scratching, and writhing, booming their misery. There's nothing to do but rebathe them, change their sheets, sop up their tears and console.

Now I know one more fact of life: itching powder really works. In fine print on the packet I read that it's made from the leg hairs of tarantulas.

I don't yet know that my husband's business will fail, that the BMW is toast, that we'll teeter dangerously close to bankruptcy until my in-laws bail us out, that I will go back to full-time teaching, that I am headed for divorce. Up to this point in my life, it seems I've told the goody-goody's story, but that's all about to change.

For the moment, in spite of looming troubles, I believe that I have a decent grip on my life as a published writer. That life is a complicated braiding of ambitions achieved and dampened, plodding strategies, and windfalls of luck. It's like holding on to the thrashing tail of a ferocious new sentence before it's wrestled onto the page. So little certainty in where the thing's dragging you, but fascination and commitment nonetheless.

For the second time, I kiss my precious rapscallions good night.

"Please tell us one more story," they beg. "Tell us a Critter story."

The Critter is an extraterrestrial creature I invented who zooms them on intergalactic adventures and endows them with magical powers. In every episode they help the Critter vanquish a monster and rescue someone held hostage on a strange and improbable planet. Always the alien Critter, despite his superior evolution, lauds the advantages and the virtues of being human. That's probably so that he can return his Earthling guests to their ordinary lives without protest.

I am so bored with Critter stories that whenever I tell one—surely we're up to two million by now—I feel like nine-tenths of my brain is getting erased. But my children love them better than fairy tales or Dr. Seuss. Whenever my narration starts to lag or turn humdrum, they are quick to jump in. Tonight they advise me that a cape of invisibility is a weaker defense than invisible nunchakus, and so I introduce into the action a Teenage Mutant Ninja Turtle, swinging nunchakus that just happen to be coated with the invincible leg hairs of tarantulas. My audience approves.

It's late when I close the door of their room. I wish I could say that I am refreshed, but that would be a lie. I am tired, but I am something else, too. Humming, feathery. Downstairs the mantel clock ticktocks its stolid heartbeat; outside, twigs, animated by a restless wind, scratch a windowpane's insistent itch for clarity, and the house feels as still and poised as another plot about to hatch.

About the Author

Marianne Gingher is the author of four previous books, including *Bobby Rex's Greatest Hit,* which was made into an NBC movie and, most recently, *A Girl's Life: Horses, Boys, Weddings and Luck.* Her fiction and essays have appeared in various periodicals, including the *Southern Review,* the *Oxford American, North American Review,* the *Washington Post Magazine, Redbook, Seventeen,* the *New York Times Book Review. A Girl's Life* received a 2001 Best Book of the Year award from *Foreword* magazine.

The mother of two grown sons, she currently lives in Greensboro, North Carolina, and is Associate Professor of English in the Creative Writing Program at the University of North Carolina–Chapel Hill.